101 WAYS TO ENJOY RETIREMENT

DISCOVER UNIQUE HOBBIES FROM AROUND THE WORLD TO START TODAY

RAVINA M CHANDRA

RMC PUBLISHERS

Published by RMC Publishers

ISBN 978-1-7780029-0-8 (Paperback)
ISBN 978-1-7780029-1-5 (E-book)

www.ravinachandra.com

I dedicate this book to all the lifelong learners in the amazing GetSetUp community, where I have the privilege of teaching.

Your stories, curiosity, and enthusiasm inspired me to create this book to share with retirees from around the world.

ALSO BY RAVINA M CHANDRA

The Art of Senior Dating:
How to Attract a Travel Companion, Trusted friend or Romantic Partner

My Vibrant Life:
A forever Journal Capturing Your Life's Journey

TABLE OF CONTENTS

A SPECIAL GIFT JUST FOR YOU!

In '**4 Simple Steps to Create Your Perfect Morning Routine,**' you will discover:

- What a **morning routine** is and why it is essential you have one
- Why having a morning routine will bring you **more focus, productivity, and purpose to your life**
- The secret of creating a morning routine using these **four components** that will **align with your core values**
- How a morning routine can elevate your life so that you may live **vibrantly**, whether you are seeking a companion, exploring new interests, or improving your health

Go to www.ravinachandra.com/books to get it NOW

INTRODUCTION

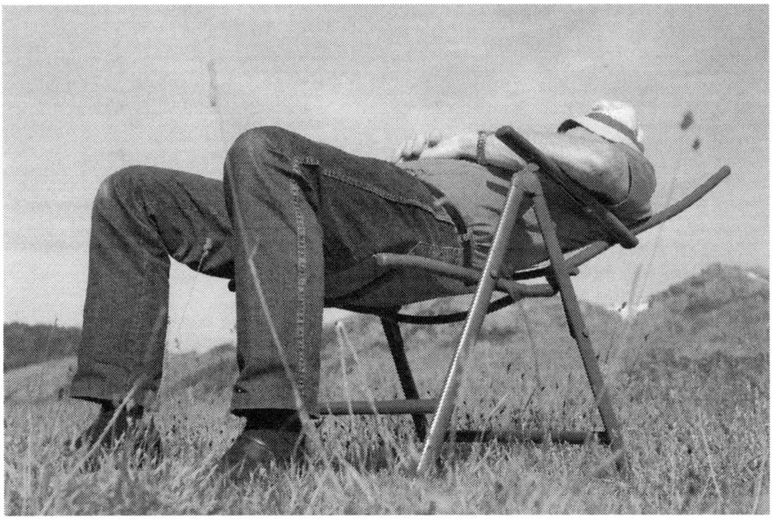

Your golden years! A chance to explore the world and try out new hobbies – or a chance to take up residence on the couch and do nothing at all?

As we grow older, our bodies tend to slow down, and we become less nimble, less flexible, and less sturdy than in our working years. But it's not all downhill.

Our brains often stay active and alert; however, we may need a little stimulation to encourage us to find the most satisfying ways to spend our leisure time.

When Harry retired, he decided that after his many years of hard physical labor, he would put his feet up and rest. And that is what he did.

He got up about midday – missing the fine mornings and fresh air. Instead, he collapsed onto the couch and stayed there in the dark all afternoon, watching reruns of tv shows he had seen years before. In the evenings, he would stir himself enough to go to the pub and drink too much.

Gradually his friends stopped visiting, even the regulars in the pub began to ignore him, and he found himself very much alone. He almost wished he was back at work.

If only – the saddest words in the English language – if only Harry had found some engaging hobbies to transform his life – if only...

Retirees from all over the world have found interests, stimulation, and exciting things to do and learn about. As you peruse the pages of this book, you will find some hobbies that are familiar to you and some you may have never heard of.

Certain hobbies might need a tweak to adapt them to your own circumstances should you decide to give it a go. For other hobbies, you will at least learn fascinating facts and a multitude of topics for you to consider. I might even go as far as saying, your travel bug within might start planning and packing its bags for your next adventure!

Some activities you can do by yourself; others lend themselves to a group, and many work both ways.

On your journey around the world, as you read this book, you will pick up some hobbies that you can start today which will also keep you evergreen, if I can compare you to a plant! You will visit countries, perhaps some you've previously traveled to, and some places entirely new to you. Either way, it will be a delight to see what other retirees around the world get up to in their spare time. Hopefully, you will be inspired to take up a thing or two yourself!

I have been in healthcare my entire career, and many of my clients are older adults – such a captivating age group. In general, they are engaging, thought-provoking, and some rather inspirational. I know the difficulties age can sometimes bring, but I also know the rewards and wisdom we can gain.

So, open your mind to new experiences and start your journey into the world of 101 hobbies. As a retiree myself, although I left behind my full-time job, I have kept myself engaged by teaching and mentoring older adults part-time, to live their best lives. This includes challenging their brains, keeping curious, and being open to learning new things.

One more thing to mention before you delve into the pages of this book, as I know some of you are wondering why your country is missing.

For every chapter of this book, thorough research and interviews took place to ensure proper representation of hobbies and countries. If you would like your country or hobby featured in upcoming books, I would love to hear from you. A special shout out to my American friends. What a vast and diverse country you have. So stay tuned for your own, special edition of 101 hobbies from across the USA.

Please contact me with your ideas at
ravina@ravinachandra.com

UNITED KINGDOM

What do people find to do on this small, damp, and crowded island?

Well, nowhere is far from the sea! The furthest you can get is the center of England, but no one seems to agree precisely where that is! Lichfield in Staffordshire has a plaque stating it holds the record of 84 miles – and note that the UK still uses miles (1 mile = 1.61 km).

The town of Haltwhistle in Northumberland has banners stating that this is the "Centre of Britain." Meriden near Coventry was known as the center of England since 1829, but this was found to be inaccurate when an attempt to validate this claim was made in 1920.

VISITS TO THE SEASIDE

This universal closeness to the coast means that visits to the seaside are popular, and they suit any age group. You can find almost deserted and stunning cliff-top paths; some are long distances which can take several days to complete, with camping or B&Bs on the way.

But for many, it's simply a day's outing, fish and chips by the sea, ice cream, and other seafood delicacies. Or maybe the trip is just a chance to walk the dog at the local beach.

Note that in some places and at some times of year (even in July), you will go to the beach wearing wellies and macs – and still have a great time buffeting the wind, hearing the screaming seagulls, and braving the icy blast, because...

...there is the pub to warm up in, have a pub lunch, chat with the locals, and learn the latest gossip. Oh, and for those who are confused, wellies and macs are just rubber boots and raincoats.

DRINKING, BRITISH STYLE

Now, talking about locals, when a Brit says "down to the local," they mean the pub.

Pubs in the UK are as unique and different in their clientele as they are in their architecture and atmosphere. There are pubs that are literally hundreds of years old; others are modern, sophisticated metal and glass palaces; but they are all places to meet, drink (another favorite British pastime), and catch up with the latest.

If you visit Britain, a trip to your 'local' will add color and flavor to your visit.

What else do the British find to do in Britain?

TEA DRINKING

In the old days, say fifty years ago, an "afternoon tea" was a feature of English life. You would have strong brown tea, brewed in the pot, then served with milk (always pour the milk in last!) and with it you'd enjoy small sandwiches and – if you were lucky – a piece of Madeira cake.

This has generally been superseded by a mug for every occasion. It is an essential aid for the workmen, the all-important comforter in times of grief or stress. A "cuppa" is still the first line of help in everyday life.

And tea goes further with the increasing consumption of herbal teas, amongst which is chamomile tea. The ritual of making a warm cup of chamomile tea just before bedtime is said to help you get off to sleep gently and easily.

Serve your guests with a tea of your choice, in a pretty teapot, with a stunning home-knitted tea cozy to keep it warm! (An elephant design springs to mind – the trunk over the spout?) This would cement any friendship, and if they reciprocated, you would have a nice little club going with the possibility of meeting new, interesting people.

GO ON A HISTORICAL OUTING

The National Trust and English Heritage are organizations that look after beautiful, rare, and historical sites throughout Britain, and Northern Ireland has a Heritage Trust Network as well. This means that everyone can enjoy a day visiting ancient monuments, lovely gardens, and historic, grand mansions.

If ancient ruins and castles are your main interest, then the heritage sites give a better choice, but the National Trust is the best option for stately homes and gardens. The Scottish Heritage and Welsh Heritage sites allow reduced rates for English Heritage club members.

Wherever you live, there will be fascinating places to visit.

FINE DINING

One popular pastime for mature people is "fine dining clubs." Not only do you get to enjoy a culinary delight, a stay in a nice hotel – often in magnificent surroundings and with pleasant gardens – but it is also the perfect opportunity to meet like-minded people, to engage in intelligent conversation, or even to meet a new partner over candlelight, for long-term friendship or romance.

These dinner parties are suitable for singles as well as couples – and the myths about English food being inedible are simply not true!

Maybe there is a similar club near you? If not, why not start one with a few close friends?

SIGHTSEEING AND PHOTOGRAPHY

Of course, the magnificent scenery is a huge bonus. Scotland and Wales both offer mountains, but these locations are often relatively isolated, so you need to know what you are doing. The saying *"Hope for the best, but prepare for the worst"* is very applicable to venturing into the hills.

The weather is a significant factor in mountain safety: things can change very rapidly in the lonely mountains – even in the lower fells of the beautiful Lake District, England – and the mountain rescue teams, made up of volunteers, are often at full stretch when the clouds descend, and the weather is foul.

As for Northern Ireland, it has to be one of the loveliest countries in the world. If you can, a short visit is accessible from the mainland and will delight your memory bank for years.

Photography is a beautiful hobby for all ages and can enhance memories on cold winter evenings while sharing your experiences with family, friends, and others. You can file photos on your computer and make a lasting folder full of happy memories. First, use the best shots as screen savers to make you smile as they appear on screen. Then, share them with your family – they make a great conversation starter.

TAKE A FURTHER EDUCATION COURSE

England is blessed with many courses at reasonable costs. Universities, old and new, colleges and schools all offer a wide choice of further education courses. Sometimes they are held in beautiful, ancient buildings with stunning grounds. The courses are a rich source of interest as well as friendships and socializing for all ages – and once you have retired, there is no pressure to pass exams! So, get your local leaflet from the library and jump in.

SPEAKERS' CLUBS

English is the language of England and also the primary language spoken in Scotland, Wales, and Northern Ireland. However, those countries also have their own languages: Scottish Gaelic, Welsh, and Irish Gaelic, respectively. So, it's not unnatural that speakers' clubs have developed to promote the use of spoken language.

There are two main speaking organizations in the UK, the International Toastmasters, with its headquarters in the United States, and the Speakers Association, which is UK based.

Both organizations promote excellent speaking skills – and in both, the meetings take on a similar format. Prepared speeches are presented, and an evaluator gives friendly guidance, praising the good points and encouraging improvements. Timing is important, and a traffic light system helps the speaker adjust their speeches to the required length. A topic session, where off-the-cuff short speeches are given, often follows a short break, and a business session might end the meeting.

New members are always welcomed. You can join just for fun, or you can follow the educational pathway the association's structure can provide. You might even go on to participate in competitions at national or international level, but many members just find the interesting topics and friendships made enough reason to join.

So, if there is a club near you – why not give it a go? It can be a tremendous boost to your self-confidence.

SUMMARY

Little "Great Britain" is packed full of beautiful places to see, every step you take is on historic ground – and the weather isn't quite as bad as people often say.

Visit the seaside for a day's outing, which might mean beachcombing, fish and chips, ice cream, or walking. Then, head down to the local (pub) – a great place to meet up, catch up, have a drink, and socialize.

Start a tea-drinking club. Visit heritage sites, and perhaps join a heritage organization. Try fine dining clubs, where you can enjoy culinary delights, meet like-minded people, have intelligent conversation, make new friends, or start long-term relationships.

Enjoy beautiful scenery by sightseeing the beautiful countryside. Indulge in a good camera and try your hand at photography.

Be a lifelong learner: take a course at a renowned institution – several offer online learning, which might suit you wherever you live. Or you could join a speakers' club.

Day trips to the sea
Drinking, British style
Tea drinking
Go on a historical outing
Fine dining clubs
Sightseeing and photography
Take an educational course
Speakers' club

THAILAND

Thailand offers lovely scenery, beautiful beaches, and charming people. Sea sports, swimming, scuba diving, and kite surfing are all available in Thailand.

Indeed, there is the exuberant nightclub life in the tourist cities, and Thai food is world-renowned for its delicious and delicate flavors.

But there are also reflective activities where calmness and focus on the present moment are given the time necessary for us all to lead a full yet pleasant life.

Thailand has so much to offer, so let's have a look.

SOAP CARVING

Have you ever tried to whittle a piece of wood, hoping to create a recognizable cat or elephant or anything else? If you have, you will know how difficult it can be to get the results you imagined, unless you have a lot of luck or a great deal of talent.

But a solution is at hand! Thailand is famous for its beautiful and elaborate soap carvings. These carvings are something quite special, but with a bit of patience, some practice, and the right tools, you could produce your own masterpiece.

But first, let us look at how soap carving came to Thailand. In the 13th century, Sukhothai had been the historic capital of the Thai Empire for nearly 150 years. People used to carve fruit and vegetables, but it all changed when a king's servant wanted to make her decorations for the Loi Krathong festival stand out. During the festival, decorated baskets were floated on the river. This unnamed servant carved a flower and a bird out of soap to brighten up her basket. And a tradition was born.

Children are often taught soap carving in school, but the real experts produce amazing, fantastical, and elaborate works. The most common objects carved are traditional flowers and dragons, all in incredible detail.

So how do you start to make your own incredible carving? The steps are as follows:

- Find a soft, inexpensive soap for your first attempts! Rectangular soaps are easier to control than round ones.
- Collect together cutting instruments. These can include a small, sharp knife, a toothpick, and even forks and spoons.
- Lay newspaper underneath your work area to collect up the scraps, which you can remold into usable soap.
- Get rid of the manufacturer's mark by scraping it off under running water, making the soap soft and easier to work.
- Make your design and etch it onto the soap – a toothpick works well.
- Scrape away the outer parts to get the rough outline and then pay attention to the detail.
- Finally, gently polish the soap using your fingers or a paper towel.

And there you have it – a perfect gift for your favorite person. Once you become more skilled, why not use scented soaps, different colors, and of course, nice packaging for a beautiful gift, lovingly made?

YOGA

Yoga is a popular worldwide phenomenon in Thailand, and many people take up this hobby and give it the respect and practice it deserves. And what better place to practice yoga than on a sandy beach with the sea gently lapping at the shore? Thailand offers its share of lovely landscapes, calm waters, and hilly getaways. Some temples add a sense of serene reflection to yoga, and there are many retreats and workshops, perhaps including meditation, which allies itself so well with yoga.

Thai practitioners have a unique "SomaVeda" way of yoga, combining spiritual and religious additions from ancient practices, incorporating traditional Thai and Chinese medicine, and also including modern science and medicine.

Thailand has a vibrant yoga community and highly skilled teachers, and places to practice with stunning views.

You can do yoga almost anywhere. However, if you intend to take up this as a hobby, you might also like to create a tranquil place in your own home where you can peacefully get into a calm state and focus on getting the best out of your yoga. Many now do yoga by watching instructions online. But there are likely yoga classes to attend in your vicinity, too.

You may also decide that a weekend yoga retreat, such as they have in Thailand, would be a superb way to start, and meeting like-minded people is one of the benefits of such a retreat. This would be a wonderful way to get away, treating your mind and body well.

Yoga is far more than just exercise. It strengthens and stretches your muscles, making them supple and flexible while creating a space for calm reflection and mental healing.

And it is harder than it looks!

COLLECTING AMULETS

This unusual hobby is popular in Thailand. There are huge markets devoted just to amulets, and department stores may have an entire floor just for them.

Thailand has a Buddhist majority, so collecting religious objects is something many Thai people like to do. And the value of these objects can rise into thousands of dollars if a well-respected monk blesses them.

Many collectors are proud to show their friends their delightful objects, although one of the most successful collectors keeps his collection well hidden in velvet-lined boxes in a vault. They are treated with respect, for they are valuable and beautiful.

Amulets might be very ancient and show the marks of time. Some may be embellished with jewels and the glitter of gold. Amulet collections are full of mystery. Who owned them? Where do they come from? Are they ancient artifacts, or were they made just down the road?

Many retirees collect things; it is just something people do. As children, we collect shells and rocks, and maybe Pokémon cards. Sometimes we continue to collect as adults: stamp collecting, for example, is a worldwide and interesting hobby. Coins and comic books are other potentially valuable and interesting collections. Other people collect such things as "do not disturb" signs, spoons, water pistols, and knitting patterns.

When you start collecting stamps, perhaps you may be delving into the history, finding fascinating facts about your past, and even building up a valuable asset to pass on to your children. People may travel the world to find that rare stamp or that extraordinary coin. So it may be worth looking over your childhood collections; just maybe you will find an 1840 Victorian "penny black" from England – the first stamp ever produced.

If comics are your interest, keep them in mint condition to hold their value, just as the amulet collectors in Thailand keep their beautiful collections.

There is an infinite number of things one can collect, and the amulets of Thailand are just one example of a relatively unusual and interesting collection.

SCUBA DIVING

You may already go down to the sea with a snorkel and flippers. Even with just these items, you can see so much hidden from the surface view, but if you want to delve deeper, then Thailand is a perfect place to learn how to do it – the safe and proper way.

Thailand offers some of the best scuba diving in the world. With the warm seas, shallow areas near beaches, and safe diving sites, it is not surprising that scuba diving in Thailand is famous, and many Thai divers are very skilled.

This is a sport that needs proper training and equipment. The island of Koh Tao offers courses for people to reach the Professional Association of Diving Instructors (PADI) certification, and there are just so many beautiful places for a beginner to explore.

I should emphasize that we are not talking about cave diving, which is one of the most dangerous sports in the world, as was demonstrated in 2018 when a boys soccer team and their coach were stranded in a deep cave that was flooding. The fast-approaching monsoon added dangerously to the water levels. The best cave divers from Britain, Australia, the US, and China, plus the superb Thai navy seals, managed to rescue them ten days after they went missing, in an epic rescue operation, which claimed the life of one of the rescuers.

Instead, we are talking about diving at a gentle pace after training and preferably in warm seas under optimum conditions for a new look at what is under the waves. Scuba diving is addictive, and you need to be reasonably healthy to be safe.

But even with just your snorkel and flippers, you can add value to your dip in the sea – you never know what you may find!

THAI COOKING

One cannot leave Thailand without sampling its cuisine, and there are many online courses available to teach you, step by step, to make some fantastic meals to astonish your friends and family.

Thai food reflects the history of Thailand. Many years ago, people from southern China emigrated to Thailand, bringing their culinary influence. In olden times, the Buddhist religion determined their choice of food. They ate a mainly plant-based diet with the addition of seafood. Meat was only eaten in small quantities – strips of meat were flavored with spices and herbs or shredded after cooking.

It was the Portuguese missionaries who first brought spices to Thailand in the late 1600s. A lady called Maria Guyomar de Pinha influenced Thai cooking. She was of mixed Japanese Portuguese-Bengali descent and married Constantine Phaulkon, a Greek adviser to King Narai.

So Thai menus owe much to their global origins, and they appeal to many people around the world today. Despite these complex origins, Thai cuisine does not have to be fearfully elaborate, and you can produce delightful meals quite easily if you know how. Add a few candles and flowers for a perfect or romantic night at home with people you care about.

If you consider yourself a foodie, like my husband and I do, then having a hobby of adventuresome cooking might be right up your alley. You could start with one type of food like Thai and build your repertoire as you circle the globe. I am sure your friends and family won't mind being your taste testing group.

SUMMARY

Thailand is a beautiful country with some beautiful hobbies. Carving with soap, you can create unique and lovely items without the physical pressure needed for carving with wood.

Adventuring under the sea is just as fascinating as exploring on land, and scuba diving in Thailand seems the natural thing to do. Courses are available at most beach resorts, so you can go scuba diving safely and explore the best underwater places.

All around the world, people are doing yoga, and Thailand has some scenic places to get out your mat and do a spot of yoga. So many people benefit from the controlled movements and serene mindset; it seems a shame not to try it yourself.

Collecting amulets is rather special: amulets are historically intriguing as well as often very beautiful. But people collect just about everything, from acorns to rare stamps. Maybe you can find something collectible that stirs your interest?

Who hasn't eaten Thai cooking? It's a favorite with many people, and if you can cook up a delicious Thai menu, your guests will be impressed. But why wait till you have visitors?

Soap carving
Yoga
Amulet collecting
Scuba diving
Thai cookery

BELGIUM

As you may know already, Belgium is famed for its chocolate, sausages, and beer.

HOT-AIR BALLOONING

Are you surprised to see hot-air ballooning is popular in Belgium? The Belgian Balloon Trophy is an annual event attracting competitors from far away. The air is filled with colorful balloons drifting across the sky; it's balloon festival time!

And many other times, when you are walking in the forests, driving along the splendid motorways, or hurrying along the pavements in town, you may look up and catch a glimpse of a balloon sailing by, high above in a clear blue sky.

A balloon ride

Many companies arrange balloon rides during the summer months, and it's exciting to anticipate what the ride will feel like if you've never been up in a hot air balloon.

Surprisingly, you often need to get up very early in the morning since the air in the balloon must be hotter than the outside air. The outside air has to be stable as well, and during the day, the atmosphere heats up and creates thermals that destabilize the air.

You arrive on site in the half-light of early dawn. You find the balloon on the ground, tethered and tugging at the ropes. A fire has been lit beneath the canopy; the air heats up, the balloon pulls harder – it's time to get in the basket.

You climb over the sides of the wicker basket; you can feel it jumping around a little as the balloon seems impatient to start the ascent.

The ropes are released, and you start to rise.

You can hear the flames of the fire heating the air; you can feel a breeze. It's still early, and the air outside is cool. You gaze over the side as the ground recedes; soon, you are floating gently over the landscape, over the fields, above the treetops.

You can see the shadow of the balloon on the ground below, keeping track with you. Maybe you pass over a farmyard and set the dogs barking. Perhaps you are sailing over the top of a town and can see the tiny cars below you. It all seems far away – all your cares are distant. For a brief while, life flows naturally around you. It's exhilarating and calm at the same time.

All too soon, the journey is over, and you arrive back at the start field and land with a bump.

Mind you, you don't always land exactly where you set off! The balloon is at the mercy of the wind, and steering can be almost non-existent.

How high you fly will depend on local regulations, but most will reach around 3,000 feet. The wicker baskets contain between two and eleven passengers and are designed to be light and slightly flexible. Hot-air ballooning is the safest form of air travel, so apart from the bump as you land, your journey should be smooth and comfortable.

You will need to research whether there is a hot air balloon club available where you live. If not a full-time hobby, it is certainly worth investigating as a fun outing, at home or on your next visit to Belgium.

GHOST HUNTING IN BELGIUM

Belgium has no shortage of abandoned buildings and haunts for ghosts. So, let's look at a few of them:

The Abandoned Castle – Miranda Château

This is a lovely building, falling into decay. Originally built by French émigrés fleeing the guillotine, this would be a haven for ghosts.

Unfortunately, this building has been neglected since 1991 and is now threatened with demolition. But it is the perfect place for ghost hunters.

Haunted House in Sas-van-Gent

This haunted house was famous and, in its heyday, attracted ghost hunters from all over Europe.

Local legend has it that a German soldier was electrocuted nearby, and his ghost haunts the house. Four Canadian soldiers joined him when a mine in WWII destroyed their tank.

This house has now become something of a legend. Rumor has it that doors slammed, cameras misted up, watches stopped, and cell phones became inactive when ghost hunters visited this haunted house. But now, we'll never know since the house was demolished in 2011 for health and safety reasons.

The John McCrae Bunker

In WWI, John McCrae wrote a famous poem that starts like this:

In Flanders fields the poppies blow
Between the crosses, row on row,
That mark our place; and in the sky
The larks, still bravely singing, fly
Scarce heard amid the guns below.

We are the Dead. Short days ago
We lived, felt dawn, saw sunset glow,
Loved and were loved, and now we lie,
In Flanders fields.

In 1918, he died while looking after wounded comrades. The bunker where he was working has become a WWI memorial site and is said to be haunted by his ghost. Visitors have heard the echoes of gunshots – and some even claim to have seen the ghost of Alexis Helmer, to whom this poem was dedicated.

The Lady of La Roche

Once upon a time, there lived a nobleman in the castle of la Roche. He had a very beautiful daughter called Berthe.

He decided to hold a tournament for the lady's hand in marriage. Among the competitors was Count of

Montaigu, although he was already engaged to another lady, Countess Alix de Salm. He seemed to be winning every joust – until the very end when a small knight in black armor killed him and took Berthe to the bridal chamber.

The following morning, Berthe and the black knight were found dead at the foot of the cliffs below the chamber's window.

The black knight was discovered to be Countess Alix de Salm. She had made a pact with the devil. She wanted to kill her cheating fiancé and the lady who was to become his wife. And now, her ghost haunts the castle.

The castle hosts ghost events, parties, and fireworks – and these events are very impressive.

Bruges' Legendary Haunted House

In 1498, there was a nunnery in Bruge and a monastery on the opposite side of the river. It had to happen – a young monk fell in love with Hortense, one of the nuns. He found a secret under-the-river tunnel and paid her visits, but Hortense rejected him and tried to escape his clutches. In a rage, the monk stabbed her to death and buried her. Now both their ghosts are said to haunt the area – Hortense clothed in white and the monk seeking her to beg forgiveness – but he can never find her, and at midnight, both ghosts disappear.

GARAGE SALES

In Belgium, they do things on a grand scale. These are not just your typical little garage sales: the whole village turns out their belongings for sale in their front gardens, in their driveways, and on the pavement. The police put out warning notices, and homemade adverts litter the highways for days ahead.

From fresh garden produce to antique butter dishes, books, and toast racks, you can find almost anything. In addition, these sales can be a great source of old but valuable vinyl records and CDs if you know what you are looking for. Even children's furniture and toys are bargains to be snatched up. These mini markets are also a friendly social gathering and a wonderful place to catch up on the local comings and goings.

Garage saling, yard sale shopping, or flea markets as they call it can be popular all around the world. If this is something that appeals to you, definitely check out what's happening in your own community. After attending a few yourself, you might find that you are hooked and make this a weekly occurrence, both to sell stuff and acquire new finds!

PATCHWORK FANTASIES

Patchwork is a global hobby, and Belgium has its share of skilled needlewomen. These skilled hobbyists can produce unique patchwork goods, an absolute joy to see.

While patchwork is a hobby that can be enjoyed alone, it is also a relaxing way to meet like-minded men and women. Groups meet in after-school classrooms, church rooms, and other venues. Typically, with these types of clubs, there will be a break with soup, tea, or coffee and a selection of savory and sweet snacks to keep up your energy.

The conversation will be what any group of people typically talk about – spouses, children, schools, pets, weather, and health, together with the latest local gossip.

So busy are the women and men chatting away; it's almost magical how they produce such beautiful things.

Every few weeks, huge markets devoted solely to materials for sewing are set up – a focus for people from miles around to snatch up bargain fabrics of every kind imaginable. It makes an enjoyable day out as you meander your way home with bags full of promise.

One of the best ways to get supplies for patchwork is to use up scraps of material from past clothes. You can make a family quilt that reminds you of the pretty dress your granddaughter loved or the shirt your husband wore and wore until it was almost threadbare, and you finally managed to sneak it out of the closet.

Patchwork can be used to make bags and sacs and covers for boxes and books. You might also make covers for your pouf or chair and oven gloves to protect your hands. Of course, they can simply be decorative, and some of the finest examples are hangings to adorn your walls.

A patchwork gift shows thoughtfulness and care, so it is always a pleasing gift to receive. Matching and mixing the different materials is creative and results in unique articles made with love! If you have at least one creative bone in your body, patchwork might be your next new hobby!

JIGSAWS

Jigsaws are popular wherever you go. They are one way to create an amazing picture but also a way to learn about places, animals, and birds, etc. A jigsaw of an old master (famous painting) is a fun way to study art; you really can see the details of the painting when you have to put it together piece by piece.

Belgium has jigsaw groups and competitions. Individuals, pairs, or teams compete to complete a 500 or 5000-piece jigsaw, and it might take several hours. This is an excellent way to make friends, and the competing element makes it quite exciting as competing teams near the end of the competition.

How does the last piece fit?

There is a wide assortment of jigsaws in Belgium; there's even one of the Belgian flag. It's a great way to learn your way around places you may want to visit – or places you never will. You won't get lost in Bruges if you have already completed a jigsaw of a map of the city!

There is not only a vast range of jigsaws but there are also a variety of ways to store the unfinished piece without demolishing it. Framing and hanging your special puzzle is a great way to have continued enjoyment.

Why not ask your friends to join in and either complete a jigsaw together or compete to see who can finish a similar one first? Last year I joined an enjoyable Facebook group dedicated to the art of puzzling, and I competed (it was a very friendly competition) in a jigsaw jamboree over a three-month period where each participant had to complete as many 1500 piece or more puzzles in the allotted 90 days. There were weekly prizes and giveaways, and even my husband joined in the fun. I plan to participate again this upcoming year.

SUMMARY

This small country with its energetic and stoic people is full of ideas to amuse you.

The castles and ghosts, together with the pretty scenery in the Ardennes, offer many exciting outings, and for the evenings, there are patchwork groups and jigsaws to keep you entertained.

When you want to clear the clutter, why not have a garage sale? You might even make some money, which you could put towards an extraordinary trip – a balloon ride! There is truly nothing like it for putting things into perspective and seeing the world from a small distance – a marvelous way to clear your mind and enjoy a few moments of serenity.

Hot-air ballooning
Ghost hunting
Garage sales
Patchwork
Jigsaw puzzles

FRANCE – L'HEXAGONE

When we think of France, we think of chic, fashion, that peculiarly Gallic sense of independent thinking, and wonderful wines. The French are justifiably proud of their beautiful country and have found a unique way to showcase it with the Tour de France.

Every region has its own specialty. Champagne is only from the Champagne region (whatever any other labels may say). Another example is the Roquefort classic blue cheese made from ewe's milk from Roquefort. Both names are protected by law – at least in France.

The scenery varies from the pink flamingos in the salty marshes in the south, where over 60,000 flamingos migrate, to the sophisticated, sunny beaches of Cannes and Nice, where the luxury yachts dock. Then there are the old hunting forests of the kings and the highest mountain in the Alps, Mont Blanc.

So, let's take a tour with the Tour de France, which visits many areas of "l'Hexagone," as the French people like to call their country.

THE TOUR DE FRANCE

The Tour de France is an incredibly arduous race. It all started in 1903 when two sports newspapers, *Le Vélo* and *L'Auto*, were in competition. L'Auto formed after disagreements between journalists about the "Dreyfus affair," which resulted in the execution of an innocent man for treason and divided France at the time.

The race was intended to boost the circulation of the new paper "L'Auto," whose editor was a keen cyclist. While bicycle races were a common type of newspaper promotion at the time, the massive scale of this race was intended to put Le Vélo out of business.

The race has undergone many changes since its inception. Now it is a multi-stage race, and the winner of each stage is entitled to wear the prestigious yellow jersey for the next stage. Each stage lasts a day, and there are 21 stages over 23 days, usually taking place in early July when the sun beats down fiercely.

Historically, the person placed last had a red lantern attached to the rear of their bike! (This attracted sympathy – and a bigger check!)

Every year the route changes to showcase a new area of l'Hexagone. But the mountainous Pyrenees and Alps are always included, together with the finishing line on the Champs-Élysées in Paris.

The tour is grueling. In 1903, many riders dropped out in the first race – it was too exhausting – leaving only 24 competitors at the end of the fourth stage. During its history, infighting, underhanded tactics, and drugs have all played a part. Four deaths have occurred; one rider drowned in a river during a rest break.

So, bicycle riding is immensely popular in France, where cycling seems to be a national hobby for all ages and all fitness levels. You see kids on bikes, women with baskets of flowers or shopping, as well as young men and the older generation, all enjoying the thrill of the wind in their faces and the lovely scenery they explore. This hobby could start at any age, even if you didn't do a lot of bike riding as a child.

More and more city planners within communities are dedicated to creating bike lanes and bike-only paths throughout their cities and natural surroundings, so pick up the latest cycling pamphlet if you are intrigued with getting on a bicycle again. It seems a trend of the past few years is electric bikes, which help on longer adventures. I've even seen three-wheeler types which would be very stable if you have balance issues; it looks like these modern tricycles may be the latest trend.

BOULES OR PÉTANQUE

Another French sport is a little less arduous. Wherever you go in France, you will find people playing boules. As you enter a village there will be a group, usually of men, playing boules on a patch of land. It doesn't matter if the ground is uneven; it doesn't matter if there are tree stumps in the way; the game can still be played. But, of course, the older players have the advantage of familiarity with the terrain! There are also "boulodromes" dedicated to the sport with gravel or hard dirt surfaces.

The game is deceptively simple: a small target ball called the jack is thrown down, and with larger balls called boules, players aim to either hit the jack, land close to it or dislodge their opponents' boule. The name is derived from words meaning "foot fixed," so the player must keep his or her feet firmly anchored to the ground while throwing. One can play solo or as a member of a team.

The game itself goes right back to ancient Greece and Egypt. In the sixth century BC, the Greeks tossed coins, then flat stones and later stone balls, attempting to throw them as far as possible. Finally, the Romans added a target, and this variation came to France with the legions.

The balls became wooden, and in England, King Henry III forbade his soldiers from playing boules – they had to practice their archery instead – while in France, the ban on boules extended to commoners – only 300 years later, in the 17th century, was the ban lifted.

Nowadays, technology has improved, and the balls are usually hollow metal boules, which are cheap to mass-produce, and they are now exported to many countries around the world. Every two years, the Fédération Internationale de Pétanque et Jeu Provençal (FIPJP) world championships take place, with the contests alternating between the mens' and the womens' competitions. But still, the best-known competition happens in Marseille, in

France, which attracts over 10,000 combatants and 150,00 spectators.

Formal games require teams of one, two, or three players. The players stand in a marked circle to throw the boules; the circles are now prefabricated 50 cm circles of red plastic often used in formal games. The number of boules for each player depends on the number in the team: in singles and doubles, each member has three boules, but in triples, each player has only two.

Points are scored for the team with the closest boule to the little wooden target, now called a "cochonnet"– and once the magic number of 13 is reached, the winning team can be announced.

There is one very odd custom. A "carreau" is a winning shot – it knocks away the opponent's boule and takes its place. But if the team scores no points, it is known as "fanny," and the losing team must kiss the bottom of a girl named "Fanny"!

Fortunately, the team comes prepared – and that explains why you may see an image or small carved figure of a bare-bottomed girl with the team.

CHAMPAGNE AND CHARTREUSE

Champagne, as we all know, is a sparkling wine that comes from Champagne in France. To gain the appellation "champagne," the grapes must be grown in designated areas, and the grape-pressing must be done in a specific way.

The Romans first planted grapes in the area and red wines were produced in Champagne before medieval times, but the first sparkling white champagne was produced by accident. Bottles exploded, corks flew out, and the wine was known as "the devil's wine!"

It was near the medieval town of Carcassonne that the first record of sparkling wine was made in a Benedictine abbey in 1531. They achieved the sparkling form by bottling the wines before fermentation had been completed.

One hundred years later, an Englishman found that by adding sugar, the wine fermented again, and in 1662, another Englishman found out how to make glass bottles strong enough to resist the bubbles.

Six years later, Dom Pérignon entered the scene with the task of getting rid of the pesky bubbles. The workers had to wear heavy iron masks to protect their faces from bursting bottles, and cellars often lost up to 90% of their bottles by spontaneous bursting! But Dom Perigean is credited with many innovations needed to produce this world-class wine, revered throughout the world.

Chartreuse

Less well known than champagne are chartreuse liqueurs, produced near Grenoble. Like champagne, the alcohol was created initially by religious communities for the taking of the holy sacrament. However, unlike champagne, chartreuse continues to be a closely guarded secret, only available to two individuals, both monks in the Grande Chartreuse monastery.

The story goes that in 1605, a French marshal of artillery to the French king, Henry IV, gave the Carthusian monks at a monastery near Paris a recipe for the "elixir of long life." So valuable was this that it ended up in the headquarters of the religious order near Grenoble, in the beautiful Chartreuse mountains. The recipe includes about 130 plants, flowers, herbs, and secret ingredients in an alcohol base. And ever since 1737, the monks have made and sold chartreuse.

There followed a somewhat checkered history. The monks were expelled from France in 1793, as were all the other religious orders. Manufacturing ceased. A copy of the recipe was made, but the monk carrying it was arrested and imprisoned in Bordeaux. However, he was able to pass the document to his friend Dom Basile Nantas. This friend believed that the monks would remain in Spain and never return, so he sold the recipe to a pharmacy in Grenoble.

Napoleon ordered that the ministry of the interior must review every recipe for secret medicine. The manuscript was sent and duly returned marked "refused." When the pharmacist died, his heirs sent it back to the monks who had indeed returned to the monastery.

The monks were expelled again in 1903. The monks took their recipe with them to Catalonia and continued to produce their liqueur. But they have now returned to France and produce green and yellow varieties of this quite sweet and spicy tasting chartreuse. And the longer the spirit stays in the bottle, the better it tastes. Today, you can take a tour of the distillery and taste the sweet chartreuse.

Chartreuse is sometimes used as an ingredient in cocktails and was on the menu in a pudding on the Titanic the night it sank. It is another example of a regional drink gaining a worldwide reputation for excellence.

Unsurprisingly in a country so renowned for its wine, tours of wine cellars, weekend wine tasting sessions, and winemaking weekends are very much in evidence. All over France, you can find workshops devoted to winemaking and appreciation, sometimes combined with golf or even ballooning.

In many countries, people can learn about wine, taste the specialties and enjoy wine in their homes. Some people store fine wines or spirits as an investment and can build up a valuable collection. It can be seen as quite a sophisticated hobby. Maybe this is for you?

PERFUME

When it comes to perfume, France is the world leader with 30% of the global market. Some of the most famous names in the industry are French, including Chanel, Christian Dior, and Estée Lauder. Chanel N°5 is perhaps the most iconic fragrance of all time. Famous perfumeries such as the Maison Guerlain are French.

One French perfume – Clive Christian's No. 1 Imperial Majesty – entered the Guinness Book of World Records as the most expensive perfume and was a limited edition presented in diamond-studded Baccarat crystal flagons.

But there is another side to French perfume. The lovely lavender fields of Provence are a riot of purples and lilacs in August. If you walk in the capital of Provence, the town of Sault, you will find everything scented with lavender – even, it is said, the roses!

Lavender has so many uses: it can be added to soaps, scented candles, little sachets to scent your laundry, and of course, lavender bags to place under your pillow to help you sleep. Lavender is also added to flavor honey and ice cream – it's everywhere.

Small lavender bags make cute little presents and are very easy to make. And if your hobby is making candles, why not use lavender to scent them?

BOULEVARD LIFE IN PARIS

What strikes a foreigner in Paris is the number of cafés on the pavements. It's a beautiful place to sip a coffee and watch the world go by – and nearly everyone does it.

These cafés serve as a social meeting place, a place to relax and unwind, and often provide meals any time of day as well as a nice glass of wine.

The French take coffee drinking to a new height. They may ask for a "grande crème" (a large white coffee), the small black espresso, or the anise-flavored "pastis." The larger coffees and hot chocolates are typically served in bowls, making them easier to dunk your croissant in!

You may see the men playing checkers or reading the newspapers. The cafés are a popular place to eat your croissant for breakfast.

The oldest surviving Paris café is the Café Procope, which opened in 1686. Cafés like this didn't always have a good reputation: before the French Revolution, they were seen as "the ordinary refuge of the idler and the shelter of the indigent."

But things have changed. In the hurly-burly of a busy city, these cafés are little oases, offering a chance to sit back, meet friends and see the world passing by. It seems to me that enjoying a coffee at your favorite café, especially if it allows you time to people-watch, read the paper and converse with old friends, would be considered a satisfying life-long hobby most would appreciate.

SUMMARY

France has some stunning scenery, and what better way to showcase it than a long and arduous cycle ride? You don't have to compete in the Tour de France to enjoy a bicycle (or tandem) ride in your local country; it's surprising how far you can go.

Boules is a game anyone can take part in – strategy is everything!

France is justly proud of its wines and its perfumes. You can appreciate wines and even use them as an investment. You may not be able to reproduce the scents of Paris. Still, you could enjoy using lavender to make candles or lavender bags – wonderful gifts, especially for anyone who has trouble getting off to sleep.

Breakfast on the boulevard is a very french thing, but why not emulate them (weather permitting)? It's an excellent, relaxing way to start the day.

Cycling
Boules
Wine appreciation
Lavender bags or candles
Breakfast on the boulevard

CANADA

Canada is vast. There is a stunning range of beautiful scenery from the sea and mountains in the west to the Great Lakes and Hudson Bay in the east, and variable, mixed weather: snow and ice, hot sun, and everything in between. And Canadians know how to make the most of it. Exploring their country by camper van is a popular choice for all ages. Curling and pickleball keep Canadians fit, and for the quieter times, nothing beats a good read.

CURLING

Curling started in Scotland in the sixteenth century. Scots played on frozen lochs and ponds. In 1541, the first recorded match was held between a monk from Paisley Abbey and one of the abbot's relatives. It's good to know the monks enjoyed themselves.

But since then, curling has come to Canada in a big way; between eighty and ninety percent of curlers in the world are Canadian! Yet still, the best stones are made from granite, and that granite was traditionally mined only in the Trefor Quarry in Wales or Ailsa Craig – an offshore Scottish island. The world curling championships only permit stones made from the granite of Ailsa Craig (Craig means rock), and there is one company with the exclusive right to harvest Ailsa Craig granite to make curling stones. The world championship in 2021 was held in Calgary (and was won by Sweden).

The stones weigh between thirty-eight and forty-four pounds, including the handle, and a new stone will cost around $450 (USD), although a used one will be considerably cheaper.

Yelling on the sidelines is part of the fun. Sayings like "hurry," "hurry hard," and "clean" all have their own particular meanings. The atmosphere is electric; the stone slides with unbelievable speed, the teams race, and the audience roars.

EXPLORING WITH A CAMPER VAN OR RV

See the country in comfort, and control where and when you stop. What could be better than a camper van?

You get lovely countryside, that back-to-nature feeling, freedom to go where you like, and evenings by the campfire – all without having to erect a tent!

Canada is a free country, and almost ninety percent of the country is designated "Crown land," and usually, you can camp there free for twenty-one days if you are a Canadian citizen. However, you need to be careful not to camp on private land – always ask first!

You can often even park overnight in a shopping mall parking lot.

Since most people stay overnight in designated places, you will find toilets and hot showers, as most camper vans do not have them installed. However, portable toilets are available (though they can be smelly!)

You may prefer an RV (recreational vehicle), which does have all modern conveniences installed. Many retired people become real pros and bring their potted plants, doormats, and even the kitchen sink.

A few tips worth bearing in mind:

- Mosquitoes can be a bane if they like you. Be prepared!
- Bumpy side roads can cause chaos if your belongings are not firmly strapped down.
- Book your campsite ahead in the busy season. The best sites are often the most popular and get full – not what you want after a long day's drive.
- Nights can be chilly, so be sure to take extra layers.
- Take an old-fashioned road map in case you visit locations off signal.

Camper van adventures not only let you visit and absorb different parts of Canada but also often give you a break from your screens and phones. They can be as sociable as you please, as you can spend time outside, mixing with other campers, yet you can also be alone with nature if that is your wish.

My good friend Barb took up camping with her newly acquired camper van just a year or so ago. She recently told me that she had camped 118 nights so far this year! Most places she camps are not that far from home. She just loves retired life, calling herself "one happy camper." If the weather turns for the worse, she can stay snug as a bug inside her tiny camper home.

PICKLEBALL

In the mid-1960s, pickleball was born. Starting as a children's backyard game, it became increasingly popular in community centers, parks, schools, and retirement communities.

The story goes that three friends returned from playing golf and found their families were bored. So they thought of playing badminton, but no one could find the shuttlecock, so they improvised. They lowered the net, found a perforated plastic ball, made paddles from plywood, and took the name from the family cocker spaniel who retrieved the balls – or so rumor has it.

It is estimated that Canada now has around 60,000 players – and no wonder. The game is easy to score and not too challenging to play. It may look like tennis, it may sound like ping-pong, but it is developing into a game in its own right, not unlike badminton. It is ideal for older adults who are keeping fit.

The game is played on a court, which is smaller than a tennis court, so perhaps needs a little less energy expenditure? Players say otherwise! It is usually played as doubles, using small paddles to send the ball over the net.

The aim is to keep the ball low, below waist level, although overarm strokes are sometimes used. Huge tennis smashes are not a prominent feature of pickleball. This game needs a strategy to win, and letting the opponent make the mistakes to gain points is one crafty one! The first to reach the score of eleven is the winning team.

But there is a strange language growing up around pickleball: words like dink, erne, forex, gentleman's rally, kitchen, nasty nelson, out-of-the-jar, poach, and the more familiar lob.

Para-pickleball (played from a wheelchair) is also becoming popular – with similar rules to the parent game. It seems this energetic game requires mental agility as much as physical strength, so it is well suited to seniors.

LITTLE FREE LIBRARIES

These delightful mini-libraries are popping up all over Canada. They consist simply of a waterproof box with a see-through door, stuck on a pillar low enough for a child to reach, with room for just a handful of books. Often these little boxes are painted and nicely decorated.

Wherever you go, be sure to keep your eyes peeled – you can find these delightful boxes on the streets, in parks, along walking trails, and in many other places. Sometimes people gather to chat about the books they have read and advise you on your next read, so they also act as social focal points.

And what better way to encourage youngsters to read as they leave the park with a book in their hand?

You might find a little library in a train or bus station – out of the rain – and this might provide the perfect reading matter for your travels. Community centers and church porches could also be great places for a mini library.

These mini-libraries tend to be set up in moderately high-income areas, so a school counselor, Sarah Kamya from New York, decided to take the idea a step further and developed little free diverse libraries to encourage people to understand life from a different perspective. She bought books by Black and Indigenous authors – and this has taken off in a big way.

She only started in June 2020, but she has already donated thousands of books and raised thousands of dollars, helping to make Black and Indigenous people's voices heard throughout America and Canada.

Starting a little library is not too hard: a box, a pole, and a few books, and you are set up. However, if you have a mission like Sarah Kamya, then you have much more work to do in keeping your library stocked with books to support your mission.

Little Free Diverse Libraries Today

LFDL is now a non-profit organization that aims to spread diverse books through the little libraries. This can inspire deep conversations about some of the issues which face us all. The aim is to expand the number of mini-libraries, especially in places where the need is greatest.

But for anyone wanting a book to read, what could be easier than plucking one out of the mini box? It can be a great pleasure for those who have too many books to pop them in the box and know that someone else will get delight from reading them.

SUMMARY

Canada has such a range of stunning scenery – and such a range of weather as well. Of course, exploring the beautiful scenery by camper van makes sense, but you could also range afar in an RV and see new places in comfort.

Curling and pickleball are both games to play or to watch, and when you feel the need to settle down with a good book, what can be better than having access to a little library, even if you have to make it yourself?

Curling
Camper van or RV exploration
Pickleball
Mini libraries

GREECE

Picture Greece, and what do you see?

Whitewashed buildings and blue-domed churches? Beaches and islands and ancient ruins? But did you know that 80% of Greece is made up of mountains? Greece is one of the most mountainous countries in Europe.

And the Greeks don't call themselves "Greek"; they prefer the name "Hellene."

Greece has an impressive coastline. In addition to the mainland, the country consists of over 6000 lovely islands, 227 of them inhabited, collectively comprising almost 10,000 miles of coastline with blue seas and stunning views.

With their hot summers and outdoor lifestyle, hobbies tend to be based on the sea or mountains – and yes, you can ski in Greece in the winter, using one of the 117 ski lifts.

You could visit an ancient monument in the morning, laze on the beach all afternoon, and take a stroll up and down the main street with the locals in the evening.

SWIMMING IN THE SEA

There is nothing quite as refreshing as a swim in the sea, and the waters around Greece are pleasantly warm. In the early morning, you might have a little cove all to yourself, and it's a wonderful way to wake up. In the afternoon, a dip in the sea is relief from the hot sun. The dolphin is the national animal for Greece, so if you are lucky, you might see them frolicking around.

The island of Santorini has different colored beaches – red, white, and black – due to the volcanic activity. And you never know what you may find. There are ruins under the waves – cities long awaiting rediscovery – and maybe in the shallow seas near the beaches; you will find echoes of the past. You can even wade out to the ruin of the ancient city of Epidaurus and see a Roman villa, or you could take a kayak. Warm waters, breath-taking glimpses of the past, and a welcoming taverna on the beach – what better way to spend an evening.

One word of warning about sea bathing in Greece – shoes or sturdy sandals will prevent your walk in the water from ending with painful sea urchin spines embedded in your feet!

TAVLI ON THE SIDEWALKS

In Greece, you can't miss the men sitting sipping their ouzo or coffee, playing board games on little tables outside the cafe.

The commonest game is "Tavli" – which is Greek for board. This can be played by families, although it is more typically the men who play.

There are three commonly played games of Tavli: Portes is a little like backgammon, with slightly different rules, Plakoto is more like checkers, and Fevga is another variation on checkers. The games date back thousands of years. So you are never far from ancient history in Greece.

Greeks play the games one after the other, for three, five, or seven Tavli points. The game is played fast, with one dice to be shared and picked up quickly, but if you throw while the opponent is still holding their piece, then you are penalized. It can be quite nail-biting.

This game is addictive. And in the pleasantly cool evenings, what nicer way to spend the evening hours than with friends playing Tavli outside the local cafe in summer.

OLIVE APPRECIATION

For over 6000 years, olives have been grown, harvested, and pressed for oil. The earliest evidence of olive farming is in the eastern Mediterranean countries. Now olives are grown in many countries and on every continent except Antarctica.

Greece is the third-largest producer of olives – about 2.2 million metric tons every year – second only to Spain and Italy, but Greece claims to grow more varieties.

Most of us know there are green and black olives, yet there are actually 139 varieties. Ninety percent of them are pressed for their oil; the other ten percent we see on our tables and decorating our pizzas. All olives start off green and slowly ripen to light brown, reddish-purple, and finally to the deep black we all know.

Like fine wines, olives all have their own unique flavor, which is influenced by the variations in cultivating, harvesting, and processing, even within the same grove.

Olive oils may be produced from a single variety or a blend from two or more different ones. As a result, there is a lot to learn about olives and their oils.

Just to emphasize the importance of olives to Greece, the patron saint of olives is Athena. Why was she chosen over all the other gods? Athena is the goddess of warfare and wisdom. To win the people over, she used her wisdom to give a gift they could not refuse – an olive tree. The Athenians thought this a better gift than that of water offered by Poseidon.

ANCIENT HISTORY & MYTHOLOGY

Greece is the cradle of Western civilization, so museums and ancient ruins are popular places to visit for Hellenes and tourists alike. Greece has over 500 archaeological sites, most of which are open to the public. Greek history is intrinsically linked with the myths of the ancient gods.

Famous sites include the Parthenon in Athens and the Temple of Apollo at Delphi, which was once home to the famous oracle. In the eighth century BCE, pilgrims came from far and wide to ask the Oracle of Delphi, the high priestess known as the Pythia, to foretell their future. Before undertaking any major scheme, the oracle would be consulted.

Mount Olympus is the home of the gods; it is the highest mountain in Greece and has 52 peaks and deep gorges. That sounds like plenty of room for the gods to think up their mischief.

The highest point is 9,570 feet, one of the highest peaks in Europe. People go there to admire the rich diversity of plant and animal life. Many birds use Greece as a stopping point on their annual migrations.

The scenery is stunning, and you can find Christian monasteries in awe-inspiring locations, including the highest orthodox chapel.

Greece has many museums with priceless artifacts from the ancient world as well as a vibrant modern artistic culture. Studying the myths of ancient Greece or other ancient civilizations and relating them to history is a very satisfying way to spend many hours.

BIRD WATCHING

Greece is placed at the crossroads of Asia, Europe, and Africa, so it provides shelter and rest for many species of migratory birds and has its own varied bird population. The Greek Ornithological Society works hard to protect endangered species, making it possible for birds and people to live in harmony. Holiday birding tours are popular, taking in some of the most beautiful scenery in the world.

Four hundred and forty-nine bird species have been spotted in Greece, and there are 196 areas designated as special for birds; these include wetlands, lagoons, and lakes. Wind farms have been prohibited in certain areas to protect the birds.

The best times for seeing the birds in Greece are when they migrate, which occurs in late April to early May in the spring, and the first half of September in autumn. And if you want to see the lesser white-fronted goose, go in November!

You may be lucky enough to see some spectacular birds, such as hundreds of Dalmatian and great white pelicans and greater flamingos – an awe-inspiring sight. To help vultures, the Hellenes provide vulture feeding stations; you may catch sight of Egyptian and griffon vultures.

Greece has a rich local bird population that includes species such as the masked shrike, Riuppell's warbler, and the spur-winged lapwing. Over 100,000 waterfowl winter on the Evros Delta, and there are many other bird-watching delights in Greece.

The good news is that bird watching can be done anywhere by anyone. Very often, there are local bird watch groups you can take part in. Gone are the days of people stealing eggs from wild birds' nests (Oology was considered a hobby where collectors collected bird eggs, but this is now illegal in most places); in the present day, it's all about conservation and ensuring our grandchildren can wake up to the dawn chorus.

Bird watching may encourage people to get up early and enjoy nature at its best before everyone else comes along. Groups can provide social friendships, lectures, and books that can increase your knowledge. Some apps translate the bird's song for you, so you know which elusive bird is singing its heart out to you.

And if you slow down the bird's song, very often, you will find a complete concerto there in all its amazing structure.

SUMMARY

In Greece, you are never far from the water, so swimming in the sea comes naturally. If you can make it one of your hobbies, it will both reward and refresh you.

Tavli are popular board games played on the sidewalks, and you could bring out your own board games and play with your neighbors on the street or in a park.

Greece is also famous for its ancient ruins and its mythology. Studying the gods and their many foibles would be a fascinating hobby, while studying archeology, with site visits where possible, could lead to many interesting conversations with fellow enthusiasts.

We don't typically pay much attention to olives. Yet, they have their own characteristics, and you could soon be an olive expert.

In many, many countries, bird watching is popular. Greece is at a bird migration crossroads, and there are many spectacular birds, some rarely seen. But bird watching is a hobby you can do in your own backyard and get hours of enjoyment, or the birds may lead you to explore new places and meet other birders.

Swimming in the sea
Tavli
Olive appreciation
Mythology
Ancient history
Bird watching

NEW ZEALAND

You will meet many active octogenarians in New Zealand. There seems to be no limit to the number of hobbies they have.

One unique characteristic of New Zealand culture is the contribution of the Māori culture. The Māori are the Indigenous Polynesian people of mainland New Zealand (Aotearoa), who originated with settlers from East Polynesia and arrived in New Zealand in several waves of waka (canoe) voyages between roughly 1320 and 1350.

Another unique characteristic is the country's pride in being self-contained, with its people trying to avoid contaminants and invasive species from the outer world, preserving their unique environment and way of life.

New Zealand is a beautiful country with stunning scenery and a pleasant climate, making it an attractive source of inspiration for many hobbies. Let's look at some of them now.

ECO GARDENING

Gardening is BIG in New Zealand. The temperate climate, the fertile soils, and the energy of the inhabitants make gardening one of the favorite pastimes for people of all ages. As a result, almost half the population indulges in gardening.

New Zealand has a vast range of bird and insect life, and many of its indigenous plants are also unique. However, since Europeans settled in New Zealand, they brought with them many plants, and some of them, like old man's beard and morning glory, became invasive.

Now there are extremely severe penalties for anyone attempting to bring seeds or plants into the country.

Ayrlies Garden

Ayrlies Garden is quintessential New Zealand. Starting in 1964, the countryside was then a bare paddock with heavy clay soil. Now, this six-star garden is one of the delights of New Zealand. It covers 12 acres and has informally planted borders plus lawns and waterways. There is also a wetland area for aquatic life and birds.

But let's give it a little twist and save the world! An ecologically designed garden uses local plants, minimizes waste, and avoids unnatural pesticides and chemicals. It needs intelligent and possibly innovative ideas to make the garden productive and environmentally friendly. Many gardens in New Zealand keep these principles in mind.

Stop digging!

Digging disturbs the microorganisms that live in the soil. So why do we need to dig? For countless eons, worms have been doing a very effective job – we should just let them get on with it. Mulching instead is much easier on your back.

Plant a tree

Warm are the winds in the woodlands
Wafting their way through the leaves.
Weaving and winding and whispering
Like wind flowing over the sheaves.
– Anglo Saxon poem

If you have room, plant a tree. Trees are decorative and provide shade and perches for birds. Beneath a tree is a wonderful place to lie and gaze up at the sky through the pattern of leaves and branches.

Research the best plants and where to put them. Some like the sun, others shade, some like clay soil, others like sandy soil, some like floods, and others prefer to stay dry. It's fun learning about your locality and how to make your garden fruitful.

Recycle

If you can use recycled goods to make your fences and pathways, go for it. Also, unusual containers for potted plants can be decorative and add a talking point to your hobby.

Grow your own food

New Zealanders excel at this. Nothing is more satisfying than tasting that first home-grown raspberry or potato. You may have been eyeing that tomato for weeks: too small, still green... ready at last! And any excess can be preserved for the cold winter months.

Leave room for the original inhabitants

Man has been busy pushing out every conceivable type of wildlife and stealing their land, their sources of food, and their shelter. We owe it to them to make provision for them in our eco-gardens. And watching the antics of a squirrel or hearing the song of the birds can provide hours of entertainment.

Let a little part of your garden go back to nature – you will be surprised at the variety of pretty plants that take over, where dead wood provides homes for many insects, and what wildlife begins to move back in.

And it's all labor-free!

BEEKEEPING

Do you need a little helping hand with your garden? Why not try beekeeping?

One of New Zealand's most famous men was a commercial beekeeper – Edmund Hillary – the first man to stand on the top of Mount Everest in 1953 with Tenzing Norgay.

In 2019, there were 9217 registered beekeepers in New Zealand with over 800,000 hives. While many of these were commercial enterprises, this figure still suggests that beekeeping is a popular pastime.

Beekeepers in New Zealand subscribe to a voluntary code of conduct, which aims to ensure the sustainability of bees. This is important since bee populations have suffered, and the numbers have declined worldwide because of the use of toxic insecticides.

New Zealand is home to 28 species of native bees, and of these, 27 only occur in New Zealand. The other one also lives in Australia and somehow posted itself across to New Zealand, unaided by humans. These native bees are tiny – only 4 - 12 mm long – so they are easy to miss. They are also solitary creatures, nesting in the ground, but there are a lot of them.

Better known are the imported honeybees and bumblebees, which are bigger and better for commercial pollination. Altogether that makes 41 species of bees you can find in New Zealand. And it's these imported bees that beekeepers look after.

Before embarking on beekeeping, you need to understand what you are getting yourself into: there is a steep learning curve. You will need to enroll in beekeeping courses, not only to learn about bees but also to help establish your bee colony, and to provide you with the support of like-minded people afterward.

The bees will pollinate your garden and make your crops flourish, but we need to take care of them and protect them from the harsh chemicals that so many of us spray on our plants.

CANNING

When your garden is full of fantastic fruit and vegetables, it would be terrible not to use them. So, preserving by canning or bottling is popular in New Zealand.

Open kettle canning

This canning method is still prevalent in New Zealand. It involves putting hot food into a jar or can and then sealing it in without further treatment.

There is no current legislation in New Zealand covering home canning. However, there are stricter rules in America, where this type of kettle canning is considered unsafe, and all guidelines in America recommend processing after canning.

It is possible that *E. coli*, salmonella, and listeria can survive in unprocessed jars.

Methods of canning have evolved to make it safe, and if you decide to preserve your garden's produce, you will need to ensure you follow the recommended procedures and recipes.

You can buy proper supplies for canning and bottling, together with the lids. If you are considering buying supplies to preserve your produce, buying in multi-packs can save you money. Because the cost of jars is high in New Zealand, many people tend to reuse commercial containers.

. . .

Memories from an old-timer

"...we were able to sit down to peel them, then pack the peeled peaches into the jars while they were still raw. Then we poured a syrup of sugar and water over them, almost to the top of the jar. The perfect seal was placed on, and the screwband tightened just right. Then six jars were placed on a wire grid at the bottom of the preserver, with a seventh in the middle. Water was added to cover the jars by at least two inches, then the element was turned on, and the water was brought to the boil. After it boiled, a thermostat kept the water just at the boiling point for the required time. Twenty minutes for peaches..."

You can find plenty of information if you are interested in preserving your garden produce. It's ecologically satisfying and can give you and your family delicious homegrown fruit and vegetables.

BOARD GAMES

Board games are popular in New Zealand, and often people combine a board game with a night in with friends. Here are a few of the popular games:

Scrabble

Scrabble is prominent in New Zealand. It is great for spelling and vocabulary and is a very mentally stimulating game.

Pictionary

Pictionary is for all ages – and anyone with a sense of humor! It doesn't matter if you are not "artistic."

Monopoly

Monopoly started out as a teaching tool to show the dangers of concentrated land ownership, but makes for an exciting challenge with friends and family.

The Game of Life board game

In this game, the player can make choices as they move through life's challenges, so it is an excellent game for older people.

Cluedo

Do you like to solve a murder mystery? A game of logic, Cluedo is all about finding clues to find out "whodunnit."

There are many other games, but the New Zealand tradition is to invite other people into your home to play. It's better than being glued to the television.

BOOK CLUBS

In New Zealand, almost everyone belongs to at least one book club. Usually, people get together to discuss a book they have all been reading.

It does mean you have to get a copy of the book and maybe read something you would not have chosen yourself, but you can often get a brilliant surprise. Together with the visit, the coffee, and the biscuits, this can be an enjoyable and educational way to spend a few hours.

Often the book club extends into such things as garden visits, exploring different varieties of trees, and tasting unusual apples or pears. Recipes and tips for around the home, and lovely personal touches are special too. Or it can be formal and strictly about the book, maybe with someone reading part of the book, or perhaps a poem. You can sit back and enjoy the sound of their voice without distractions.

Some of the clubs have a theme – maybe, for example, animals or train engines – which can lead to exciting outings for members. Book clubs are as versatile as their members.

There is also an extensive range of virtual book clubs, so you can make friends with people from faraway places with a common interest. In addition, people living in a foreign country may find a book club is a great way to establish friendships with like-minded people, and improve their foreign language acquisition.

U3A

To continue with slightly academic subjects, many New Zealanders are members of U3A – the University of the Third Age. This will keep those grey cells active.

This started in Toulouse, France, and has spread all over the world. Some of the groups might be loosely attached to the local university, but more often, they are started by people who want to know more about life. And who better to tell them than the older people who have lived it.

Usually, people meet every month or so, and one of the local members or maybe a visiting expert will give a talk about a subject that interests them. It could be about their career, but it could equally be about their hobby.

The range of interesting subjects is infinite, and because the speakers themselves are enthusiasts, the way they impart their knowledge is often exciting as well as informative.

Often there will be a break for tea or coffee and a chat. You can meet some fascinating people here, folk who are intelligent and experienced in life. And you do not have to give your own little lecture unless you want to.

True words from Peter Laslett of U3A Cambridge, 1981, founder of the UK branch:

> *"Those who teach shall also learn.*
> *Those who learn shall also teach."*

U3As provide lifelong learning and sharing for retired and semi-retired people. Taking part might encourage you to step a little out of your comfort zone to take part in active learning and contribute.

Sometimes, mini-groups branch off, where people with particular interests can share their thoughts and knowledge. Examples might be art, archaeology, modern history, travel, and many more. These groups require an administrative backup – a committee, including a secretary, treasurer, newsletter writer, and organizer.

U3As may be run quite differently. For example, in France, the meetings tend to be led by working academics.

However, in Britain, a more egalitarian approach was favored, focusing on self-help, which is usually the model followed in New Zealand.

CHOIRS

People in New Zealand love to sing together. Most New Zealanders have sung in school choirs, and more and more people are joining choirs as adults, rediscovering the joys of singing together. In fact, it is not unknown for people to join three choirs at once.

But there is more than just the joy of participation: there is the opportunity to excel for those who want it. National choirs like the New Zealand Youth Choir and the Voices New Zealand Chamber Choir have won international awards. Many ensembles travel overseas to sing. Soloists may also become world-renowned.

The New Zealand Choral Federation organizes an annual festival and competition for the choirs of secondary schools called The Big Sing. It lasts three days – and involves a tremendous amount of preparation and many, many rehearsals.

The pleasure of joining in, of taking part, producing some brilliant sounds, and perhaps even the possibility of winning competitions, makes joining a choir something the people of New Zealand love. Might there be a local choir in your neighborhood to sing with?

CROCHET CLUBS

Finally, for a more peaceful occupation, there are crochet and knitting clubs. There are many groups scattered all over New Zealand. It's not just a chance for a good natter: it's also about the sharing of skills and the final production of that gorgeous sweater or that cute little toy.

But it wasn't always quite so peaceful. Take the case of Henry Coutts. Queen Victoria herself crocheted four woolen scarves, which were awarded to four colonial soldiers for gallantry. While working in South Africa, Coutts risked his own life to rescue a mortally wounded non-commissioned officer from the Burmese Mounted Infantry. For this deed of valor, he received a gold star and clasp, plus one of the Queen's own crocheted scarves.

And don't think crochet is just an old lady's hobby. Take the case of Lissy Cole and Rudi Robinson-Cole's life-size crocheted wharenui (communal house of the Māori people of New Zealand.) This was inspired by Maori design, and the idea is to help people understand mātauranga Māori or Māori knowledge. This is an ongoing project and is expected to take over two years to complete. They hope to involve many Māori people in the work as well as international and local artists. This will spread joy in our lives, derived from Māori culture and insights.

Many charities, especially animal charities, are crying out for little crocheted or knitted toys to either sell or let the animals use as toys. Likewise, children's charities often desperately need gifts with a personal touch for children in need. Some charities want knitted blankets; there is a wide range of charitable concerns for people with the skills to help.

Crochet and knitting clubs are versatile, friendly places for people to share a pleasant few hours in the company of like-minded, artistic people, and no two clubs are exactly the same.

SUMMARY

New Zealand is full of people actively enjoying their many hobbies.

Eco-gardening not only cares for the planet but can also provide you with healthy food. And keeping bees to pollinate your crops makes good ecological sense, although there is a steep learning curve for new beekeepers.

And once you have grown your food, why not preserve it? Canning and bottling are both popular methods in New Zealand, and there are plenty of instructions on the internet to help you get started.

Then we have three activities to keep your brain supple. First, consider board games – there is a huge variety – something to suit almost anyone. There is U3A – the University of the Third age – if there is a group near you, join it for interesting talks and conversations. New Zealanders also enjoy book clubs – are there any near you? If not, why not create one?

Choirs not only let you sing, but also connect you with your fellow singers. The joint effort creates a great sound as well as gives a person a sense of belonging. And if all this is too much, how about joining a crochet group and producing some unique articles as well as having a good chin wag?

Eco-gardening
Beekeeping
Canning and preserving
Board games
Book clubs
U3A
Choirs
Crochet clubs

GERMANY

Television, radio, and surfing the internet have become increasingly popular ways for Germans to spend their leisure time. They are also great travelers, and if you meet a hardy tourist in an out-of-the-way place and wearing top-notch gear, the chances are he or she will be German.

Germany is a land rich in legend, with the secretive Black Forest and the beautiful Bavarian Alps. So, let us explore the things the German people like to do now.

TATORT

The Germans have organized a slightly different slant to watching television. Since 1970, a program called "Tatort" has been running continuously. Tatort means crime scene.

Around ten million Germans tune in every Sunday evening because it's more fun to watch it with company. Pubs have often organized public viewing sessions, and many participate by tweeting, in addition to watching and discussing.

It's a clever concept since different regional broadcasters take turns to produce the episodes, so the action takes place in different cities. That's one way to get to know your country.

RIVER CRUISES

Another way to know your country is to take a river cruise. And floating along the blue Danube or the river Rhine has all the delights you could wish for.

So, let's look at river cruises. These are smaller and more intimate than grand ocean liners, but they often provide a high level of comfort. Being closer to the scenery, you can get a good idea of the country you are passing through.

The beautiful blue Danube

You could travel along the Danube, which starts in Germany's Black Forest and, 1,785 miles further on, ends up in the Black Sea in Romania. It passes through four capital cities (Vienna, Bratislava, Budapest, and Belgrade) and is surrounded by the home cities of great composers like Mozart, Brahms, Beethoven – and of course, the Strauss family. You likely know "The Beautiful Blue Danube," the immortal waltz by Johann Strauss.

River Rhine cruises

Germany also offers river Rhine cruises. The river winds its way between fairy-tale castles perched on impossible cliffs and visits medieval towns on its way. The Rhine Gorge, the river's central section, has achieved World Heritage Site status.

There are mysterious legends as well as stunning scenery and historical interest to entice you. For example, Siegfried, the great German hero, allegedly slew a dragon on the shores of the river Rhine, and Lorelie, the water nymph, lives beneath the surface. And for decades, the river was the boundary between the Roman Empire and the barbarian hordes outside.

Some of the places you might visit include Strasbourg, with the soaring cathedral and the quaint canals; Cologne, for gothic spires as modern skyscrapers, as well as Koblenz with its dominating fortress.

Christmas cruises

Christmas cruises are special. You can sip your warm glühwein (mulled wine) with the scent of cinnamon as you watch the towns lit up for Christmas along the bank of the river. Then, stop off at a Christmas market, where you can buy all you want for a festive celebration. Snow sets off sparking lights, and as darkness falls, the air seems magical. You will likely hear carols or maybe sleigh bells as Father Christmas visits.

GEOCACHING

Geocaching is a fairly new outdoor activity that has taken off globally. It's a treasure hunt with a modern twist.

Geocachers give clues for those seeking the "treasure," or geocache, a small, waterproof treasure box hidden somewhere outdoors. The modern twist is that every geocache also has global positioning system (GPS) coordinates, which get the treasure hunters to within 50 feet.

Today over 1.4 million geocaches have been hidden, and over 4 million people worldwide have taken part in hunting them down. And Germany, together with America, is a world leader.

This can be an exciting outdoor activity, and anyone can take part; you might go solo, do it as a family outing or join a small group. You might compete with others; there are many possibilities. And you learn about new places as well.

You need a GPS and a waterproof bag to collect any rubbish. There are strict ecological rules:

- The geocache must not be buried anywhere where it might cause damage or harm.
- The geocache must be safe – no knives or explosives, drugs or food.
- Local regulations must be respected, and local signs obeyed.
- The local environment must not be altered.
- People should not need to cut back vegetation or disturb nesting sites to find the treasure.

The most popular geocache in the world is in Prague, in the Czech Republic, but Germany has a fantastic site in

Baden-Württemberg, which offers a five-stage multi-cache – quite a challenge.

Entry is often free, but it does take time and expense to set up a cache.

TOY VOYAGERS

The inspiration for the toy voyagers was from the film *Amélie,* which featured a traveling gnome. Could toys go places, see the world and meet people?

This has become a global community for toys and their hosts in various countries, including Germany. There are over 6000 members, and more than 3000 toys have been sent on their travels to 148 countries.

Hosts offer places for the toys to stay, but toy hosts do more than that: they give their little guests a guided tour of places of local interest, take photos and post them on the toy's own travelogue.

You can put in requests for toy hosts to send your little toy too, and your toy may then be returned or sent on further adventures.

To give your toy the opportunity of a lifetime, register him or her with ToyVoyagers.com. You can also browse the travel logs of other toys, and it can be fascinating to follow the adventures of these little travelers.

Once registered, your toy will have its own travel log, which its hosts can update. And if it has its own bucket list, maybe there will be a host out there happy to help.

It's an excellent way for you to travel the world without any of the discomforts, delays, and documentation associated with travel.

GARDEN GNOMES

"Gartenzwerg" is German for "garden dwarf," but the biggest gnome is nearly 18 feet tall! Most garden gnomes are a more manageable size of between one and two feet tall.

There are about 25 million garden gnomes in Germany. Originally they were manufactured in Germany, but the gnomes are now often imported from China or Poland, and there is a huge variety in type and price. And if you think they can be slightly brash, know that they were originally made to decorate the gardens of wealthy people in Europe and are now popular with all social classes.

Their history is a surprisingly ancient one. In Rome, an idol of the god of fertility was often placed in gardens. During the renaissance period, Paracelsus described gnomes as "diminutive figures two spans in height who did not like to mix with humans." Garish stone statues, including the Gobbo, or hunchbacks, adorned (if that is the right word) the gardens of the rich.

Then, in the 1700s, these little folk became entwined with the legends of Germany, and many were thought to bring good luck to farms and mines. In Dresden, the first ceramic dwarves were created in 1841 – possibly the first actual garden gnomes?

Their popularity rapidly spread, and one early gnome, called "Lampy," produced in England, is now on show at Lamport Hall and is insured for £1 million! Yet, for a time, gnomes were banned from the prestigious Chelsea Flower Show in England.

Snow White and the Seven Dwarves created a surge in interest and lower prices. And the gnomes might travel as well: there was a "hobby" of stealing a gnome, taking a photo, and then returning the gnome plus a photo to the owner. Another kind of toy voyager!

You can find every kind of garden gnome, although traditionally, they are bearded males. Many are funny, slightly grotesque, or even evil-looking. Take your pick, but collecting garden gnomes can be strangely satisfying and it can make for an entertaining walk with your grandchildren to go see the gnomes.

SUMMARY

Germany is a land of legend but also very modern. The hobbies reflect this dual personality.

Taking inspiration from Tatort, communal watching of television shows turns a solitary occupation into a fun social gathering.

Another modern twist is the geocaching treasure hunt. This can take you to places you might not otherwise even know existed.

But going back in time, river cruises take in some remarkable scenery and extraordinary castles, each with its own legends. And if you don't fancy a river cruise, you can bring some of the mythology into your own backyard by installing a dwarf or three.

Toy voyaging is yet another way to explore the world by sending off your toy to do the hard traveling – they will be well looked after by other toy voyaging experts.

Tatort
River cruises
Geocaching
Toy voyagers
Garden gnomes

AUSTRIA

Austria has a rich and varied history together with beautiful mountains in the south and rich plains in the north. Cycling, family walks, and eating out are some of the ways Austrians spend their free time.

Arts and crafts are popular, and Austrians produce lovely homemade jewelry. Singing, dancing, and music echoes off the hills. They yodel in the mountains; in their leather shorts, they dance the Schuhplattler with energetic knee-slapping. They engage in folk music with accordions and a double-necked guitar, and of course, there is the legacy of the immortal Mozart and the renowned Haydn.

Vienna is known as the City of Music: composers lived there, stayed there, and wrote awe-inspiring music in Vienna. There are many venues for concerts and theatre, and Vienna is also famed for electronic music.

Here are just five of the many hobbies available.

THEATRE

Vienne and Salzburg are sophisticated cities with many concert halls, opera houses, and theatres. Each has its annual festivals, lasting several weeks.

The first Salzburg Festival Hall was set up in 1925 in an archbishop's stables. Salzburg was the birthplace of Wolfgang Amadeus Mozart, and both music and drama were featured there. One of the highlights is the annual performance of the play "Jedermann" (Everyman) by Hugo von Hofmannsthal.

Vienna has the Burgtheater (the Imperial Court Theatre), the national theatre of Austria, one of the most important theatres in the German language and has a checkered history. It was originally built in an old tennis court in 1540 and was re-opened in 1741 by the empress who wanted a theatre next to her palace. It was then relocated again in 1888, destroyed by American bombing in 1945, and rebuilt once more in 1955. The Burgtheater has developed its unique style and is considered to be at the forefront of German theatre.

But newer musical traditions have also arisen in Austria. In 1967, the first international annual hip hop festival was started in Salzburg. This festival features new works and attracts local and international hip-hop artists.

But what could be nicer than a group of friends visiting the local theatre? You have an opportunity to dress up, a chance to gossip and catch up on the local scandal, and even to improve your mind.

There are so many local theatre groups putting on shows and wanting audiences. Sometimes the outing can involve overnight stays and a chance to make new friends and store up a good memory to look back on.

YODELING

Yodeling is fun but not something to be practiced in your living room unless you live a considerable distance from anyone else!

In Napoleonic times, yodeling in the Tyrol Alps in Austria was used as a gesture of defiance to the French troops. Meanwhile, yodeling became assimilated into folk music in neighboring Switzerland, and festivals were organized to celebrate local traditions.

In both countries, yodeling was seen as patriotic, especially in Nazi Austria. Switzerland was eager to produce its own brand of yodeling to differentiate it from any others and distance itself from the Nazi ideology.

In the 1960s and 1970s, yodeling was seen as somewhat ridiculous, but a revival has taken place, and yodeling is now a popular pastime. It is undoubtedly a great way to relieve stress and communicate with other people at international workshops.

And yodeling carries a long way – one can imagine a leather-shorted mountaineer yodeling across the valleys to a friend on the opposite side.

I'm not too sure what a spouse or partner will think of you taking up yodeling, but I will leave it to your own discretion. It sounds fun to me!

ACCORDION PLAYING

When you visit Austria, you will meet an accordion player, whether you like it or not. Invented in Austria, this versatile instrument is the backbone of traditional folk music, especially in mountainous regions.

The traditional Austrian Schrammelmusik ensemble is made up of accordion, guitar, clarinet, and fiddle. You hear them in country fairs; you will see them on local parades; and in the evenings you can watch them on stage accompanying folk dancing. Orchestras in Vienna developed their own kind of blues, "the Viennese Blues," in which the accordion played enthusiastically.

Naturally, there are accordion festivals, including one in Vienna where 200 accordionists meet and play for a month of varied music on various accordions – the squeezebox, the concertina, or even the hand-organ.

The accordion is loud. It is also versatile and has a happy sound – it makes you want to smile, get up, and dance. I have vivid memories of myself with my friend Cindy, learning to play the accordion from her family members while visiting Europe. We had such fun; we were full of smiles!

JEWELRY MAKING FROM SCRAP (OR KITS)

Austria is home to some beautiful hand-made jewelry, but it's not all made from scrap.

Schullin's studio is just one of the places in Austria where you can find modern designs made using traditional crafting methods. This family business has been operating since 1802.

They start with the rough stone and customize the finished item to the buyer's personal taste. They even use digital 3D modeling to ensure the piece is perfect.

But nearly anyone can learn to make jewelry, and you don't need to buy expensive supplies. Instead, you can buy kits with readymade beads, gems, silver wear, and all the tools you need to make breath-taking jewelry pieces.

More challenging and possibly even more engrossing is making jewelry from scrap. It's amazing what you can do with a safety pin and a sample of material or homemade paper beads.

It's still best to make sure you have the tools you need to cut wire and thread strings.

Your hobby provides you with unique and thoughtful gifts or items you will be proud to wear yourself. You might even be able to sell them, although that is a tough market to enter.

The concentration needed and the focus required are wonderful ways to alleviate stress, and it doesn't take up much room in your home.

SUMMARY

This cheerful little country is also the venue for music, theatre, and artisans producing beautiful jewelry.

You can make your own jewelry from scraps, and the only limit is your own imagination.

Learning to play the accordion could be interesting – it's loud and cheerful, and why not yodel? Who can make the best sounds in your family? (But in both cases, be wary of annoying your neighbors since these sounds are meant to travel.)

For something a little different, you could always emulate the Schuhplattler dance.

But for a classy evening out, the theatre can be an elegant and social occasion.

Theatre groups
Yodelling
Accordion playing
Jewelry from scrap or kits

SINGAPORE

Modern Singapore was founded in 1964, but its past extends to the 7th century when Buddhist-Hindu empires made their homes there. It is a tiny island off the southern tip of Malaya, which you can drive all the way across in half an hour. Its name means "lion city" in Sanskrit, although there were never lions in Singapore.

Although the official language is Malay Bahasa, the government uses English for official communications. However, many of the locals speak "Singlish," a local combination of languages derived from English with additions from Chinese and Teochew.

Singapore has some amazing sites crammed into such a small space, including the famous Gardens by the Bay, the inspiration for the film Avatar. Lit up in red, blue, and purple lights, it attracts thousands of visitors.

Despite its relatively short history, Singapore, with its six million inhabitants, has grown rapidly from a poor agricultural country without industry or natural resources to being placed in the top ten wealthiest countries globally. Business is incredibly efficient, and the people of Singapore have turned this strategic shipping point into a worldwide technological innovation hub.

So what do the island people do in their spare time?

JOURNALING AND BLOGGING

Life is fast-paced and can be stressful for many people. Journaling is an excellent way to relieve stress and also keep a record of your life. And if you feel comfortable sharing your thoughts, blogging is also a great option to keep connected with the world around you.

There are many different forms of the journal, and in Singapore, you can find them all. A favorite seems to be the bullet journal or "BuJo." This usually has sections for your to-do list, calendars, recording your health and exercise, plus a written section for your goals. Keeping track of how you feel and your actions are conducive to good time management – a feature of the efficient people of Singapore.

Singaporeans have paid workshops to help people make the best BuJo they can. They explore the concept of journaling, its presentation, tools you might find helpful, and what to do when you make a mistake.

But there are many other types of journals. You can share them, communicate through them or just relax on the couch with them. Some examples might include:

- Project journal
- Travel journal
- Diet journal
- Dream journal

And there are many more.

Keeping a journal can help you "see the forest for the trees." It's so easy to forget what is important to you, and a journal can remind you why you get up in the morning.

One tip is to buy a nice book to write your thoughts in – it makes it special.

Blogging comes naturally when you live on a small, crowded, yet prosperous island. Singapore has a multitude of blogging websites, and some of them are very well known. Blogging can be a great way to express yourself as a hobby, and you can add in social media to market your blog if you wish to do so.

Digitalization has transformed the way we communicate worldwide, and Singapore has taken full advantage of this. Of course, you need skill and perseverance to create a successful blog, but what a wonderful way to meet all kinds of people from all over the world online. You can share your recipes – like the hot chili crab of Singaporean fame – you can moan about just about anything and debate with people thousands of miles away or just next door.

Common topics include health and beauty, films and media, and travel. In fact, there is something for everyone from this tiny land.

VIRTUAL REALITY

Singapore is one of the most technologically advanced and connected countries globally and is at the forefront of new and exciting digital technologies.

While nothing can beat the real thing, a virtual reality, or VR experience can get you pretty close nowadays. Internet and virtual reality cafes are popping up all over Singapore, opening up opportunities and experiences to individuals of all ages.

A computer isn't necessary; you may need to invest in some electronic hardware, but even some newer smartphones can do the trick on their own. Your local community might even have some VR cafes so you can try things out before making an investment, and not have to bother with the technical end of things yourself. VR headsets slide over your eyes and block everything else out, so make sure you have a comfortable and safe area available!

Before you know it, you will be attending virtual concerts, touring famous museums, and seeing priceless exhibits in locations far from home. And it doesn't have to just be by yourself: these virtual experiences can also be enjoyed with family, neighbors, or friends from around the world.

Make it a group event to attend virtual workout classes, enjoy relaxing meditation experiences, or visit favorite childhood landmarks. Having a virtual meet-up with family overseas can feel like you are all in the same room together again.

Or, if mobility is holding you back, you could relive experiences from your youth that your body is no longer up for, like playing a demanding sport or going on a safari. And if you're feeling more adventurous, you could try things you would never have imagined doing in real life, like scaling the highest mountaintops, skydiving, or bungee jumping, all without the danger.

COLLECTING PLASTIC BAGS

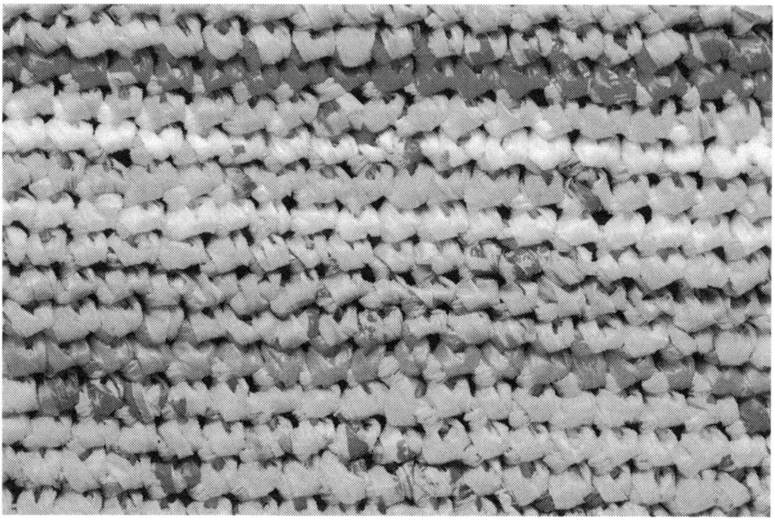

This might not sound like a fun hobby, but plastic kills marine animals and birds and damages our oceans and environment. With Singapore's small size, they are conscious of their limited landfill space, and thus recycling is encouraged.

Despite some limitations in their recycling program, there are places in Singapore that accept plastic bags and other junk for craftwork. This is where collecting plastic bags can become an interesting hobby.

The bags come in so many colors and can be made into so many items for further use. Decorative mats and woven baskets are just two; you can probably think of many more. And as you collect the bags and recycle them, you are also doing your bit for the environment.

I am not thinking of the beach cleanups many volunteers in maritime countries engage in – incredibly useful and wonderful social occasions though they are – rather, this is collecting new or nearly new bags that would otherwise be dumped in landfill sites, polluting our planet.

SUMMARY

Singapore has a vibrant and energetic community, with some common hobbies. Common hobbies in Singapore reflect the industrious nature of its inhabitants. You might try journaling to keep your brain active and organized, blogging, perhaps to make money, but more usually to share your own experiences and knowledge and open lines of communication worldwide. Collected plastic bags can be made into various attractive and useful items, or you could choose something else to recycle into a home-made creation.

Journaling and blogging
Virtual reality
Collecting plastic bags

ITALY

Italy is so rich in culture that we are spoilt for choice. Everywhere there is stunning scenery from the vertical cliffs of the red-rocked Dolomites in the north to the sandy beaches and blue seas of the south, and the pastures and villages, churches, and vineyards up and down the countryside. Italy is a Catholic country, so many of the works of art are religious, and many of the finest murals and sculptures are to be found in the churches.

Italy has an enormous archaeological heritage, from the Greeks and the Romans, with some of the world's most famous art being produced in the medieval and renaissance periods. Italy has been home to incomparable artists like Michelangelo and Botticelli, along with scientists like Galileo and Da Vinci making contributions to mankind.

We are fortunate that so much of Italy's history has survived to enchant us today. Here is a small selection of hobbies and interests that are popular in Italy that you might like to try.

CHESS

You may not associate chess with Italy, but they have a different slant on it – living chess.

In the pretty hill town of Marostica, people can watch a re-enactment of a live chess duel. It all started back in 1454. Lord Tadio Parisio had a beautiful daughter named Leonora. Two noblemen both wanted her hand in marriage, so the lord organized a live chess game – the winner could take Leonora, but the loser had to take the hand of his younger daughter Oldrada (killing two birds with one stone). He held a grand parade with flags and fireworks and a great feast.

History does not record how the two young ladies felt. But ever since then, every two years, the live chess game is re-enacted on the pink and white marble slabs embedded in the center of the piazza, which form a chessboard. This event has parades, banners, and exotic costumes, as well as the game itself, and tickets to watch are a sellout.

Chess has been around for nearly 1500 years. The game probably originated in India; from there, it spread to Persia. Then, it carried on in the Muslim world and reached southern Europe with the Moorish conquest of Spain. Now it is one of the most popular and intellectually demanding games in the world.

This really is a case of use it or lose it. Playing mentally demanding games such as chess has been shown to keep our brains in working order, so it's an excellent hobby for older people with the time and patience to work out strategies and tactics and the competitive nature to outwit your opponent.

If you can't find a chess club or local competition, you can also play against a computer. Even the computers play against each other in the World Computer Chess Championship. But as a hobby, chess can be stimulating and relaxing. What could be nicer than settling down with an old friend or with your grandchild for a friendly game of chess?

MOSAICS

Mosaics are an art form requiring the placement of small pieces of colored glass, minerals, shells, tiles, stones, or other materials closely together to form a pattern or picture. Walls and floors can be adorned in this way, and the multifaceted art can result in a shimmering and quite stunning image, which seems almost alive.

The oldest mosaic we know of dates from the third millennium BCE in Mesopotamia, but mosaics were popular in ancient and Byzantine Roman times.

When Mount Vesuvius erupted in 79 CE, the pyroclastic flow buried the small town of Herculaneum (as well as smothering Pompeii). Among the findings is the House of Neptune, a small, richly decorated townhouse. At the very back of the house, there was a courtyard with a garden, a grotto, and a fountain. On the back wall is a stunning mosaic, in vivid blues, featuring Neptune. One can imagine the family retiring to this peaceful haven after a long, hot day to relax and unwind.

But it's the town of Ravenna where the most awesome mosaics can be seen. Among the many churches with mosaics is the sixth-century Basilica of San Vitale. Here, the mosaic is a political statement depicting the emperor Justinian as central to the church's power and the military and imperial powers.

You can find mosaic floors even in the far-flung corners of the Roman Empire. But wherever they are located, the mosaics often have a deliberate fault, for to be perfect was to challenge the gods.

Nowadays, the peaceful focus required to place the mosaic pieces with care can be a fantastic way to create lasting beauty. Mosaics do not have to be floors or walls; they can decorate small surfaces, making, for example, a beautiful and unique box – maybe using the shells from a seaside visit to make a lasting memento.

Sometimes a community project might use a mosaic to decorate a railway station wall, as in Brighton, UK, where a workshop for children is producing a colorful mosaic. So this is a hobby to share or to work on solo.

Creating the lasting beauty of a scintillating, multifaceted mosaic can be enormously satisfying. And there are kits for sale and books of instructions just waiting for people to enjoy putting together mosaics as a hobby.

HAND GESTURES

Have you ever watched an Italian talk? It's fascinating. They seem to talk with their hands. And other Italians understand what the hands are saying.

Here are a few of the gestures an Italian may use, but be aware that they are open to misinterpretation and may mean different things in different parts of Italy. Nonetheless, it can be fun to try them out with friends and maybe make up your own system of signals.

So what?

Run your fingers up your neck and past the tip of your chin.

Idiot

Fingers point to your temple – we all know this one!

What do you mean?

Put your fingers together and point them upwards. Hold out your arm a foot away from your body and maybe move your hand up and down, or hold it still.

Finger kiss

Place your fingers together. Kiss them. This means "well done."

Please help

Make a prayer – put your hands together as if praying in front of your chest.

Perfect

Press your index finger to your thumb and draw a straight line in the air horizontally.

But remember, for the Italian, these gestures come naturally – and in other countries, the same gesture might mean something entirely different. You could make up your own, or incorporate some useful bits from your country's sign language. If you make a hobby of hand gestures, it might change the way you speak!

ART AND SCULPTURE APPRECIATION

It isn't easy to know where to start with art in Italy. Everywhere you go, you can find churches with treasures in them as well as museums with priceless works of art and sculptures.

Perhaps the greatest sculptor of all time was Michelangelo, and these are his words: "I saw the angel in the marble and carved until I set him free." He felt that every block of stone had a statue inside it, and it was the sculptor's task to find it.

One cannot fail to be moved by his "Pieta" or be impressed by his David. Yet, Michelangelo is perhaps even better known for his painting on the ceiling of the Sistine chapel.

There are other tremendously gifted Italians; Leonardo da Vinci comes to mind. He not only painted perhaps the most famous portrait of all time, the Mona Lisa, but he also created an airplane that could fly (he died in 1519). His painting of the Last Supper is almost equally famous and very beautiful, full of emotion and color. Much of his work was as an engineer for war machines, but he also worked as a scientist and architect.

While you may not be able to create works of art like the great Italian artists and sculptors of the past, you can appreciate them, and art appreciation is an amazingly insightful hobby. Once you begin to study paintings, you begin to understand a little of their history, and for those of you interested in how the paints were mixed, how the canvas was prepared, and so on, there is much fascinating detail to be found.

If you go to a sculpture museum, try blindfolding yourself and then feeling the exhibits, if this is permitted. You will get a totally different sensation and feel the piece at a deeper level of your consciousness.

We are fortunate that there are so many images we can look at in books and on the internet and physically visit museums and art galleries. This is a hobby with endless possibilities and is a way of communicating with people of long ago.

OPERA

Wherever you go in Italy, you will hear people singing. From open windows, from balconies, from the gondoliers, as they move along the canals in Venice, you will listen to a full-bodied song.

When you go to the opera in Italy, it is like nowhere else. The audience is part of the occasion. It's a time to wear your best clothes and be seen. Italy is famous for opera. Many famous composers were Italian, people like Puccini, Rossini, Paganini, and Monteverde, to name just four. The most performed opera in the world is La Traviata by Giuseppe Verdi, another Italian composer.

Now imagine it is a warm autumn evening, and the sky is dark. You enter the colosseum and maybe sit far back. There are 50,000 people in the audience. There is a buzz of anticipation, then silence, and far down below, the cast appears, and you can hear every word. This is because the acoustics are so good. Real horses and camels appear on stage; the opera Aida is in full flow. And when the opera ends, as it must, the audience comes to life, as only an Italian audience can.

But not to be outdone, the Italians have devised a modern type of opera, Opera buffa (comic opera), which is funny, modern, and may even include popular tunes. This contrasts to the "Opera seria" (tragic or dramatic opera), so there is something for everyone.

Singing is a well-known way to relax and open up your heart. The Italians do it in real style, but why can't you engage in opera? You could join a club or simply listen and maybe collect opera recordings.

Singing in your bath along with the rollicking tunes or declaring your hopeless love for a damsel can be very empowering!

SUMMARY

Italy is a land of song and art, from the gondoliers singing as they ply their gondolas in the canals of Venice to the fabulous sculptures and art in Rome and Florence, and everywhere you go.

Live chess is an interesting way to play this popular game, but an ordinary chessboard, a good partner, and a lot of patience will stimulate your grey cells, which might help keep your brain young.

Mosaics are an art form we tend to skip over, yet Italy has some brilliant examples, and it is something you can easily take up using natural materials close at hand or buying kits – there are plenty of them.

The art and sculpture of Italy are awe-inspiring. You may not be able to paint the ceiling of the Vatican (although one artist has painted a reproduction in a local church), but everyone can appreciate art. Visits to local art galleries and museums, plus the extraordinary variety of art books, make this a hobby that gives endless delight.

Hand gestures are natural to Italians, but they can be fun to try to make yourself understood, and if you learn sign language that the deaf can understand, that could be a bonus.

Finally, there is the opera. In Italy, opera houses are full, and the audience participates. Live opera is an experience not to be missed. Even at home, there may be a seemingly endless supply of vinyl, CDs, radio, and digital music you can enjoy; sing along as that usually makes us feel happy.

Chess
Mosaics
Hand signals
Art and sculpture appreciation
Opera

DENMARK

Denmark is a small country, made up of a peninsula and many small islands with beautiful, sandy beaches. Danes are seafaring travelers by nature and have left their mark on many faraway places. Despite being small, Denmark claims the largest island in the world that is not a continent – Greenland – as part of the Kingdom of Denmark.

Denmark also has the longest combined rail and road bridge in Europe, five miles long, connecting the Danish capital, Copenhagen, with Sweden. And, of course, we cannot forget the little mermaid statue in Copenhagen.

So, let's look at some of the hobbies that Danish people enjoy or have enjoyed in the past.

RUNES

The Danes are a part of the Scandinavian group of Vikings, a seafaring people who traveled far and left their mark in the form of runes – Viking graffiti – which you can still find in some surprising places today.

No one knows where runes originated, but it is thought they are not older than 100 CE, possibly arising in Germanic tribes north of the Black Sea and spreading as the Goths and Huns came west. After that, runes were adopted by the Scandinavian peoples, including those living in Greenland and Iceland and the Sami of Lapland. It was the only writing we know of around 300 CE in Scandinavia, while the Latin script superseded it in the rest of Europe.

Runes could be read from right to left, from left to right, or even upside down, and as mirror images. Punctuation appears to be minimal. All runes are uppercase. But they could look very decorative when well written by a master. Maybe some of them were the magic formulae for spells and charms?

Like today, graffiti writing was a popular pastime, and the Norsemen left their mark far and wide. One of the best-known examples of their doodling is in Istanbul in the famous mosque of Hagia Sophia. Two bored Vikings left their names, Halfdan and Ari. It is not impossible that these two characters worked as bodyguards for the Byzantine Emperor. Vikings left their runes in Orkney and Scotland, and the biggest runes are found in Denmark and Sweden.

Discovering runes and trying to decipher them can be quite engaging, and there are books all about runes for anyone interested in Viking graffiti.

LEGO

Ole Kirk Christiansen worked as a carpenter in Billund, Denmark. He began making wooden toys around 1932 to supplement his income, and by 1934 his company took the name of Lego, which translates as "play well" in Danish. The original blocks were made from wood.

Soon after, Christiansen imported the technology to make injection-molded plastics. Lego has been plastic since 1949, but modern developments keep the company ahead as a world leader in producing toy building blocks.

In Denmark, you can spend two or three days visiting the workshops and getting an inside view of how Lego is produced, and you can see inside Christiansen's original house. You can meet the Lego workers and designers. There are exhibitions of Lego sets and original models, and you can even take part in building your own unique design.

In 1968, Legoland Billund resort opened – a theme park built entirely of Lego. And now there are theme parks in many parts of the world: Europe, North America, the Middle East, and Asia. You can visit the Arc de Triomphe in Paris; you look down on Big Ben and Buckingham Palace in London; there are many other famous places you can see – all in miniature, all made from Lego. You can also enjoy exciting attractions and water rides in a Lego theme park. It takes millions of bricks to build a Legoland park, and what an interesting job, designing and maintaining these exhibits.

But you don't have to go out of your home to enjoy Lego. You can get creative with a box of mini bricks, mini engines, and your own imagination or an instruction manual to guide you. Who knows what you will end up with? Lego isn't just absorbing for kids: it can be an entertaining hobby for anyone.

RANDOM ACTS OF KINDNESS

Random acts of kindness occur worldwide, but Denmark has a special place in this for two reasons: hygge and escape.

How do you define a random act of kindness? It's providing unprompted help, often to strangers, without expecting any reward except that it makes you feel good. Kindness helps us as individuals to reduce stress on both giver and receiver, as your brain releases the "feel-good" hormones. Acts of kindness also help build up a sense of community and change the world we live in for the better. Nowhere are they better demonstrated than the escape of the Jews in April 1940.

When the Nazis overran Denmark, the Danes, being independent thinkers, decided to save the Jews, and over 90% of Danish Jews were deported, not to Nazi concentration camps, but to neutral Sweden, in small, crowded fishing boats. Within days, most of the Jews in Denmark had escaped. And it was ordinary Danes who cooperated in hundreds of small acts of kindness. This was an awe-inspiring feat.

The Danes continue to cooperate in kindness today, and farmers are required by law to put aside 5% of their land to grow field flowers for the bees.

Is it so surprising, then, that according to the World Happiness Report, Denmark is in the top three happiest countries to live in? The Danes have a concept, "hygge," built into their character and hard to translate. It roughly means finding comfort, pleasure and warmth in simple, soothing things. This concept spreads beyond the Danish shores, which is a surprise to many Danes since it is integral to their character. They use the word "hygge" in everyday speech without thinking about it.

With their excellent work-life balance, Danes have time and energy to do things they enjoy, whether that is knitting socks or running around the block. Hygge has a unique meaning to everyone.

But you don't have to be in Denmark to start a random act of kindness! These lovely acts are happening everywhere, and even a smile can be a gift to a lonely or sad person. Sometimes, the giver asks the receiver to pass on their own act of kindness to spread these good feelings.

Of all the hobbies in this book, this has to be the simplest and most rewarding.

FAIRY TALES

When you think of fairy tales, you probably think of Hans Christian Andersen. Born a poor cobbler's son, he died rich and famous. Spinning words to make multi-layered yarns, his tales have a charm and sophistication all of their own. With worldwide renown as simple fairy tales with all the aspects that children love, you may be forgiven for thinking his fairy tales lack depth, but look a little closer. You can find the hidden messages of philosophy and wisdom behind the simple translations.

The earliest fairy tales were of magic, ways of explaining and perhaps trying to placate the sometimes-hostile environment: a world where the shamans and bards had power and long, long memories. Often in praise of kings and rulers now forgotten, they encompassed all the elements of desire, fear, appeasement, and prowess of heroes and damsels. Myth and magic were inextricably intertwined with the tales of bravery and the long antecedents of rulers – now themselves lost in the mists of time.

Hans Anderson was a shrewd observer of people, and how they behaved. He was a serious craftsman: his tales are based on human nature with all its failings and heroism, set against the background of 19th century Denmark. He wrote 156 stories that have been translated into over 125 languages – you probably recognize some of them: Thumbelina, The Princess, and the Pea, and every boy's favorite, The Emperor's New Clothes. Anderson's bronze statue sits at the corner of "H. C. Andersens Boulevard," the most densely trafficked artery in central Copenhagen, Denmark.

Writing fairy tales for your own amusement or your grandchildren stimulates your imagination. For many children, going to bed involves the ritual of reading a story, and very often, they beg you to tell them your own story, and they listen with rapt attention. So why not write a few down and make your own book for them? Maybe they will pass your book of fairy tales onto their own children's children. You are famous at last!

SUMMARY

Demark is a seafaring nation, and they have left their mark in distant places, sometimes as graffiti in their runic writing. Runes can make an interesting study; you could even write your own.

The country is perhaps best known for the world-renowned Lego. Together with the add-on mini-engines, these little plastic bricks can make an engrossing pastime, and not just for children.

The grandkids will love the fairy tales you write. Hans Christian Anderson wrote many ever-popular stories, and now you could too.

But perhaps the very best hobby from all countries is the random acts of kindness, and in setting the example, Denmark is an inspiration to us all.

Runes
Lego
Random acts of kindness
Fairy tale writing

CHINA

China is a vast and beautiful country with a long and impressive history. Many of the world's inventions were first produced in China. What is most remarkable is how the mind and body are both involved in many of their hobbies.

The calm focus needed for calligraphy and Tai Chi, the relaxing effects of indoor waterfalls and Feng Shui, and its people's respect for their families – past and present – make China a country full of interest and delight.

We can only offer a snippet of their incredible range of interests and hobbies here.

FENG SHUI

Feng shui means "the way of wind and water." The very words are emotive. The art of feng shui originates in China, but is spreading worldwide, although, for a while, it was made illegal in China by the ruling communist party around 2005. Luckily it has made a comeback.

Feng shui has roots in early Taoism in the third and fourth centuries BCE.

What is the purpose of Feng Shui?

We can adjust our homes to instill a feeling of calmness to soothe our minds and nurture our bodies. It's a practical way of looking after our souls and being in harmony with our environment.

It is not a religion; it is not a belief system; it is not even superstition.

Feng shui may affect where we place our furniture, how we deal with clutter, and even the design of our window frames to make our homes better places to live in. But, if you get it wrong, it can adversely affect you, according to feng shui principles.

When you go shopping, you find that many large stores are set out in a very specific manner, scientifically tested to encourage you to spend money.

Here's an example in your home: if the bathroom door opens directly opposite the kitchen area, does it not feel a trifle unclean?

Similarly, if a coffee table has very sharp corners that you must carefully pass by every time you sit, does this feel uncomfortable or unsafe?

Keeping clutter well under control is also a part of feng shui. It feels good to lay your hands immediately on whatever it is you are looking for.

Some things you can do

You do not have to change your house or turn it sideways, but how you place your furniture, mirrors, and lighting can make a difference, and so can the colors you choose.

For example, it's said that if a doctor wants to shorten the number of people waiting, he will paint the reception area red in the hope that some patients will get too impatient and leave; if a therapist wants you to relax, the reception area will be a calm green or blue.

Windows are a key feature. It is nurturing to look outside at trees and the sky, but the right curtains or the right color frame can make a difference.

Do you need to cancel out noise with an extra glass layer? Or can you have your windows open any time of day?

Furniture placing

A sofa against a wall feels more secure when you are resting on it. It can be disturbing if people continually walk around the back of your sofa.

Can you see the doorway from your desk? When the door opens, we tend to see who is there, and it's easier if you do not have to turn your head.

There are many ways to enhance your home, guided by feng shui, an excellent little hobby to make you feel better.

INDOOR WATERFALLS

What is more peaceful than the sound of water flowing gently in an indoor fountain?

An indoor fountain can be a part of feng shui, and you can design and make them yourself. You might even make them for your friends – an unusual gift – or even sell them.

Waterfalls, fountains, and aquariums can give your office or home positive energy; make sure they are in the best place for them. They are said to attract good luck, and we all need a bit of that! Flowing water means life, enthusiasm, and helps you center yourself. And if you have air conditioning, this helps stop the air from drying out and becoming too arid.

But first, a couple of record breakers:

At Singapore's Changi Airport, in the new extension, there is the "rain vortex." This stunning waterfall is seven stories high and pumps 500,000 liters of rainwater down through the roof in a spectacular show.

But this record won't stand for long. The Eden Project is reaching out from England for its first international project in China's Shandong province. It will host the world's largest indoor waterfall, 50 meters high (nearly as high as the Niagara Falls). This Qingdao facility is an exciting project, a tremendous educational and tourist attraction for China, and a scientifically important biological environment.

To get the best results, you need to place your indoor water fountain in the right place. Choose southwest for a new partner, southeast for good luck and prosperity, and to further your career, go for the north.

When you make your own water fountain, you can beautify it in many personal ways: candles and flowers, lighting, and mirrors can all enhance your water feature.

YOUR FAMILY TREE

The Chinese have a reputation for looking after their elders, and they have a long history of ancestor searches. They have recorded their findings for nearly 1000 years, so if you happen to have Chinese heritage, modern research into your Chinese family can be very satisfying.

A zupu (also called a jaipu) is a Chinese genealogy book recording the lineage and famous members of a family.

But many countries maintain similar records; for example, births and deaths are recorded in the church registers, land changes in the title office, and people wrote about their personal journeys and kept diaries.

I remember a friend showing me around Hereford, UK, and pointing out the market cross, where her ancestor had been hanged for disorderly behavior.

You never know what you will turn up!

What Chinese Genealogy Records Exist?

Before paper was invented, records were kept on shells, bones, and bronze in the early days. People sometimes tied small objects into knots in ropes to keep in touch with previous generations.

Jaipu were the manuscripts used from around the 1600s. Even poor people revered their ancestors and kept their own jaipu. Many of these survive to this day; some are scattered, and others published, but many were destroyed in the cultural revolution of the 1960s and 1970s.

Inside the jaipu, people may find information about migration, military, and government affairs as well as praise of the worthy and encouragement for future generations to bring honor to the family.

While reasonably complete records of the males are often found, daughters might be left out, as are relatives who had shamed the family or entered a monastery.

And just in case you are wondering whether you have any famous ancestors, think about this: Genghis Khan, a mighty and victorious Mongolian warrior in the 13th century, not only conquered and ruled the largest empire in the world, but he also helped to populate the world. He has about 16 million descendants alive today!

If you decide that you would like to know more about your ancestors, there are many places you can go for help on the internet. In addition, you can buy albums to record your information and make your own jaipu.

PAPERMAKING

The Chinese invented papermaking. A Chinese court official named Cai Lun has gained credit for the invention of papermaking, although it was probably around before him. But he did introduce the idea of sheets of paper sometime around the year 105 CE.

Previously, people wrote on silken cloth, but that has its own problems and was expensive as well. Cai discovered a cheaper alternative that gave a smoother writing surface. He used hemp waste, old rags, fishnets, and the bark of trees.

From China, the papermaking sills were exported to Korea and then to Japan by Buddhist monks around 610 CE.

Nowadays, you don't have to go hunting around for old rags and the bark of trees – you can buy kits to make your own paper at home. And when you have produced your beautiful paper, you will have many uses for your paper, including handwriting your own words.

CALLIGRAPHY

Chinese calligraphy is an art form, widely practiced and respected. In ancient China, the four most sought-after skills and hobbies were:

- The board game "Go" (a simple concept but an incredibly cunning game)
- Playing a stringed instrument
- Painting (which is allied to calligraphy)
- Calligraphy itself

One could go a stage further. China is expansive and could only be ruled with the help of a massive civil service. The only female empress, empress Wu Zetian, declared that entry into this prestigious service required one to write poetry – and it was a stiff test.

Chinese characters were being written as long ago as 4000 BCE on ceramics with cinnabar paint. The characters were also inscribed on ox shoulder blades and tortoise shells, possibly used as oracle bones to foretell the future.

What distinguishes Chinese calligraphy?

There is an emphasis on motion: the writing is dynamic and seems to be moving. The time and rhythm are emphasized and offset by the use of white space.

After fountain pens came to China from the West and italic writing became popular, traditional Chinese calligraphy was used less and less. The italic script originated in the Pope's office because it is elegant and, importantly, legible. Just like the Chinese characters, the spacing and proportions of hand-written italic writing are an art.

Now we have computers, and the use of italic writing for emphasis and quotations has become so easy that it can seem a chore to hand-write anything, especially calligraphy; but the art of beautiful writing still enthuses many people worldwide. It's relaxing as you take the time to focus on each letter, as every one has to be perfect.

Calligraphy is decorative, but there are formal rules, and you need very few tools to get started.

You'll need a brush, ink stick, inkstone, and special mulberry paper to create this beautiful art. As you practice and gain confidence, your work will become more fluid and beautiful.

TAI CHI

Like so many Chinese hobbies, tai chi has a spiritual as well as a practical outlet.

It is a gentle form of slow, dance-like exercise. It is perfect for any age group, and the older person can do this without strain or stress on their bodies.

The movements are slow, your muscles are gently stretched, and your breathing deepens. You focus on the feeling of the movements as your body flows from one movement to the next without pause. Your body constantly moves but at your own pace.

You don't need special equipment. You don't need classes or company, although you will see people of all ages moving together in China, outside, in parks and squares. But you can do this on your balcony, in your garden, or any place where you feel comfortable.

The fact that tai chi is low impact makes it suitable for people who need to move without putting pressure on aching joints, and it does make a calm and refreshing start to a day.

You can practice your mindfulness if you wish, or enjoy the sky and the trees and perhaps the birds singing, just for you.

SUMMARY

From feng shui to indoor waterfalls, the Chinese have made the creation of their indoor environments into an art. Practical, physical ways to enhance the space you live in are combined with patience and respect for your inner mind.

Many of us are interested in our ancestors, none more than the Chinese. Making your own family trees can throw up some unexpected discoveries.

For an extraordinary craft item, you could make your own paper and use your best calligraphy pen to write a charming poem.

Relaxing your body as well as your mind. Tai chi is gentle, controlled, and calming – something most of us need in our busy lives. China has so much to offer.

Feng shui
Indoor waterfalls
Family trees
Papermaking
Calligraphy
Tai chi

THE NETHERLANDS

The Netherlands is a fantastic place. Nearly a quarter of its territory is below sea level, including the Schiphol international airport. But the Netherlands defenses are worthy of respect: a network of dams and storm barriers to protect this low-lying country from rising sea levels.

The iconic windmills, the tulip fields full of color, the clogs, and the cheese markets make this a special place. In addition, there are the craftspeople who produce the renowned Delft Blue earthenware and the famous Flemish old masters. And everywhere you go, there are bicycles – millions of them – for the country is flat.

So, let's explore a few of the hobbies you can find in the Netherlands.

ICE SKATING

The English word skate is derived from the Dutch word "Schaats," and ice skating in the Netherlands can be traced to 800 CE. Although, originally, the skate may have been made from animal bones. Many years later, wood was substituted for bone, and the first iron skates were made in the 1500s.

The weather used to be colder, and every winter, the waterways iced over, so skating was a practical form of transport for people and goods.

Nowadays, when the canals ice over and the skates come out, it's time to enjoy the speed and freedom of skating, plus the change in scenery that snow and ice give the landscape. Along with kiosks that sell hot drinks and snacks, ice skating is widespread, and any age can participate. In the Netherlands, thousands come out to play when the ice is firm.

The linking of skating with "koek and zopie" (cookies and hooch) goes back to the 17th century when this magical drink was created—an alcoholic and spicy concoction that includes beer, rum, cinnamon, and eggs. Now sadly, it's mostly split pea soup and hot chocolate that is served.

For those intrigued, here is a typical recipe for zopie:

3 12 oz bottles of a dark beer
1 cinnamon stick
2 cloves, whole
2 slices of lemon
1 cup brown sugar
2 eggs
4 Tbsp rum

Bring the dark beer, with the cinnamon stick, cloves, and lemon slices to a boil, then turn the heat down and simmer for about fifteen minutes. Whip the brown sugar with the eggs until foamy.

Carefully add a Tbsp of warm beer to the egg mixture and stir. Do this five more times, then take the beer off the stove. Remove the cinnamon stick, lemon, and cloves. Carefully stir the rest of the beer into the eggs in a tiny stream. Make sure the eggs don't curdle and keep stirring. Pour everything back in the pan, and return the pan to the heat, but do not let the mixture boil, just warm it up and keep stirring until the beverage thickens a bit and it looks smooth and velvety in texture.

All that is left is to stir in the rum, add some whipped cream, and a pinch of cinnamon!

The Netherlands dominates speed skating in the Olympic games, and the Dutch have won around 25% of the medals since 1924 – especially impressive given that the Netherlands is a small country.

Sadly, with the climate warming up, the skating season in the Netherlands is getting shorter and shorter. This sport has to wait for safe conditions, and you can't just take the skates out as soon as the canals freeze over. A thickness of almost three inches of ice is generally deemed safe but local conditions may vary, and people do drown every year when they fail to check.

But if your area reaches low temperatures, there is nothing quite so exhilarating as ice skating, and many areas either have indoor ice rinks all year-round or make them as the winter temperature drops. You can sometimes find them as part of the Christmas markets.

A word of caution, though, as old bones can break more easily than young ones, so don't go trying to out-speed the youth – let them win sometimes! But taken gently and with care, ice skating can be an excellent hobby for those winter days when it can be tempting to laze by the fire or under the blankets.

CHEESEMAKING

Most countries have their own famous and favorite cheeses, and the Netherlands is no exception.

With its characteristic red rind, Edam has been exported to many corners of the world for hundreds of years. You can visit the town of Edam and explore the cheese warehouses of the 1700s. Millions of tons of cheese are exported every year. And just 50 miles away is the home of Gouda, another, slightly more decadent cheese.

The cheeses are made with milk – although there are now vegan options available. Gouda uses whole-fat dairy, and Edam is made from lower-fat dairy, so it tastes slightly drier.

In the Netherlands, wooden vessels were traditionally used to manufacture cheese since metals were not locally available. They had to heat these by adding hot water as fire would burn them. To make room for the water, as much whey was removed as possible; we now call this method the "washed curd" method of cheese making. This gives the cheese its unique flavor. The cheese tends to be milder and sweeter than many other kinds of cheese.

About ten liters of milk are needed to make one kilo of Gouda cheese. First, the milk is pasteurized, and then a small amount of culture is added, followed by liquid rennet, then annatto for color.

The Netherlands has special "cheese markets," with a great variety of delicious cheeses on show. But how about making your own cheese?

There are many workshops on the internet, plus books, courses, and videos on making the perfect cheese. However, if you make your own Gouda, it usually takes about six weeks before you can taste the finished product.

There are kits with everything (including instructions) supplied, and there are vegan kits as well. So you might be able to show off your own cheese at your wine and cheese tasting sessions or simply enjoy your creations yourself.

FLOWER GROWING AND ARRANGING

The Netherlands is famous for its tulips – fields, and fields of them in the spring, full of color and depth – one of the most fabulous flower shows on earth.

Tulips came to Europe from the Far East via the spice trading routes; they were deemed exotic, and it was "bad taste" for any wealthy man to be without his own tulip collection.

The golden age for Dutch tulips was in the mid-17th century, when "tulip mania" was in season. The price of tulips was beyond that of gold. The rarest bulbs were priced at six times an average salary, or 10,000 guilders (for which you could buy a fine mansion on the Grand Canal in Amsterdam).

Of course, the inevitable happened, and the tulip market bubble crashed – one of the most spectacular market crashes of all time.

The Dutch not only produce the finest tulips, but they also know how to create some of the most innovative and exciting flower arrangements you can find anywhere. Dutch floral designers travel worldwide to demonstrate their skills, and people from many countries travel to the Netherlands to study the art of flower arranging. There are trade fairs, exhibitions, and courses available for the keen florist.

The delight of flower arranging is that you can use any flowers and greenery available to you – even the daisies on your lawn – to make lovely arrangements to beautify your home or to give as gifts.

Naturally, one has to be careful not to over-pick the flowers: in some areas, picking wildflowers is forbidden to preserve their beauty for future generations. But, on the other hand, buying flowers in season is not expensive.

Not only do the arrangements look pretty, but you also get a sense of peace and tranquility when putting them together, and, depending on how seriously you take up this hobby, you need very little in the way of equipment.

All you need is a good pair of sharp floral clippers and perhaps floral netting, tape, or sponge. To preserve your creation, try adding one teaspoon of sugar to one liter of water.

SUMMARY

Think of the Netherlands, and the image of tulips springs to mind. Flower power is very real here. But growing and arranging flowers is a hobby for anyone.

The Dutch people shine at speed skating, and when the canals freeze over in winter, out come the skates. Speed skating might not be for you, but ice rinks open up in winter, and you could have a good laugh learning how to skate.

One of the other things the Netherlands is renowned for is its cheese, and cheese making is a Netherland hobby you could copy. Many countries have their own cheeses, so it might be worth finding out about the cheese in your part of the world. If you like cheese, then this is a hobby for you.

Ice skating

Cheesemaking
Flower growing and arranging

I hope that the wheels are turning and you are thinking of ways to enjoy life to its fullest by starting new creative hobbies. I wrote this book for people just like you and me, transitioning into retirement or already into your golden years.

As a Health & Life Coach, it is important not to leave anyone out. Everyone deserves to live a vibrant life, so if this book has brought you some joy, a glimmer of hope, or a solid plan to improve upon your day-to-day, I have a favor to ask you. Please stop what you are doing right now, and go to your computer or phone and leave a review on your Amazon account or wherever you purchased this book.

Your review will greatly help other readers decide if this book is for them. Thank you for taking the time to leave a review.

BRAZIL

Brazil is immense: it takes up nearly half the continent of South America. Renowned for coffee, carnivals, and costumes, Brazil has unrivaled beaches and an energetic, party-like atmosphere.

Alongside the atmosphere of an urban festival are over 1,300,000 square miles of Amazon jungle. The Amazon is crucial to our planet, with its 390 billion trees producing a sizable fraction of our world's oxygen supply, as well as providing a home for an extraordinary amount of biodiversity. Roughly 60% of the world's rainforest is situated in Brazil, although at the moment, it is decreasing every day.

We have not yet plumbed the depths of the treasure to be found in the wild forests of Brazil, which may one day provide insights into new medicinal drugs, ecological systems, and a treasure trove of undiscovered flora and fauna.

Brazil offers a wide diversity of scenery and architecture. Life there is vibrant and energetic, never more so than dancing the samba, their traditional dance. While Portuguese is the official language, illustrating Brazil's colonial history, tribes we have never met may still be living in isolation in the forests.

There is much to discover – and much to enjoy – so let's have a look at some of the hobbies you can find in Brazil.

CARNAVAL DO BRASIL

Nowhere does carnival quite like Brazil!

Every year, the streets are filled with dancing people in fantastic and colorful costumes. Around two million people fill the streets, and the economy benefits from 500,000 visitors. It's one gigantic party.

If you have the chance, visit the Brazil carnival for a once-in-a-lifetime experience.

But even if that is not possible, there are often carnivals in many towns and villages throughout the world, and you can take part.

The floats take time to prepare, the costumes need designing, making, and altering, the band's practice marching, ideas flow, and everyone who participates is part of the team. Often the tractors or wagons need to be in perfect order; no one wants to be stranded in the middle of the parade. There are work or volunteer jobs suitable for everyone.

The noise, the excitement, the route lined with spectators – even if it isn't in Brazil, it can be exhilarating, and usually, anyone who can help, even in a small way, is very welcome indeed.

Taking part in the preparations for your local carnival can be pretty exhausting as the day draws nearer and nearer, but it is a great way to be part of your local community. And the kids love it.

It might be a time to practice your samba just like they dance it on the streets of Brazil.

SAMBA

The samba is the traditional national dance in Brazil. Brazilians dance it at carnivals and everywhere else they go.

The samba is a mixture of African drumming and European marches. The origins are rooted in the colonial slave culture: the Africans brought dance, music, and drums.

But the samba is a happy, lively, and upbeat dance. It has a rolling hip action, pelvic tilt, and a bouncy rhythm. You need to be supple to move your torso and give expression to the dance. But most of all, the samba is fun!

The dance costume varies, but the emphasis is on the elaborate headpiece allied with a bikini-style outfit or a long, flowing skirt and wrap-tie top.

Elements of rock and jazz have updated the samba, so it really is a dance for everyone.

If there are classes near you, then you are fortunate. If not, there are videos on the internet, and maybe you could persuade others to join you?

Samba is all about joy and passion. The movements are fast, but no one is watching the meticulous, well-ordered sequences – you can do it your way. And if you are a little stiff, you can move any way that suits you.

There is no need to overdo the action – just relax and enjoy the lively music and the movements you can comfortably make, even if that is only tapping your foot and watching from the sidelines.

CHEESE BREAD MAKING

Pão de queijo, otherwise known as cheese bread, is found everywhere you go in Brazil, and it is delicious and straightforward to prepare.

The cheese bread is made from cassava flour and Brazilian cheese. Don't worry if they are not in your local supermarket – substitutions are acceptable, and you can experiment to find your favorite flours and cheeses.

You can eat this anytime, but in Brazil, breakfast is often chosen as the best time to enjoy Pão de queijo. It's definitely something to get up for.

Here is a recipe you can make with ingredients from your local grocery store.

The results are soft, gooey, and very cheesy rolls. You can even freeze them.

Ingredients

- 4 cups tapioca flour
- 1/2 cup water
- 1 1/4 cups milk
- 2 large eggs
- 6 tablespoons oil
- 1 cup shredded mozzarella cheese
- 1 1/2 cups grated parmesan cheese
- 2 teaspoons salt

Instructions

- Preheat the oven to 400°F.
- Combine the milk, water, oil, and salt in a saucepan to boil over medium-high heat.
- Put the tapioca flour into the bowl of a mixer and, when the milk mix boils, pour it over the flour.
- Mix it well. It will come out white and sticky.
- With the mixer still on, add eggs, one at a time.
- Then add the cheese, a little at a time, until thoroughly mixed in.
- The dough is supposed to be soft and sticky. Add a little more flour if necessary – but not too much.
- Shape dough into balls by wetting your hands with cold water, make balls slightly smaller than golf balls.
- Place balls on baking sheet. Cover with parchment paper.
- Bake 15 to 20 minutes or until golden and puffed.

Try not to eat them all at once!

ARMCHAIR CAVING

Many countries have amazing caverns and caves – and I am not suggesting you don protective gear, oxygen tanks and descend deep into the earth's crust. Caving can be a dangerous sport and is best left to the young, supple, and expert.

However, the earth is riddled with holes of various kinds, and learning about them, perhaps making a journal about them, will lead you to find out many fascinating facts about our planet. Why leave it all to the youth? Let them do the hard work, and you can enjoy the knowledge gained.

You can explore the underground town of Derinkuyu in Turkey, where over 20,000 people once lived. You can marvel at the 30,000-year-old images of horses and bison skillfully painted on the walls of caves like Lascaux in France. You could dive deep into caves in Yucatán, explore ancient cities like Herculaneum, and you can delve deep into caves with small entrances without brushing against the giant spiders that lurk there near the entrance.

But one of the best places in the world to find "paleo burrows" is Brazil. So, to start your journal, here are a few facts about paleo burrows:

In 2008, Heinrich Frank was driving along a Brazilian highway when he noticed a strange-looking hole by the side of the road. Frank was a geologist, and he had never seen anything like this before, so he explored further.

The tunnel was elliptical and around three feet in diameter. On the walls were deep gash marks – like the claw marks of a large animal. Water could not have made this tunnel. Neither could tectonic activity or lava flows. It had to be made by an animal, and a large animal at that.

It is believed that giant sloths were at work here. Although they became extinct 10,000 years ago, they have left their mark. In fact, Frank went on to discover over 1500 paleo burrows in Brazil.

There are so many more fascinating facts to find out about in exploring our underground caverns, and you can do it all from an armchair. The internet is full of incredible cave images and videos.

However, if you get the opportunity to descend into a cave as part of a guided group, it is an experience like no other, and the experience will stay with you forever.

SUMMARY

The country of Brazil is enormous, and Brazilians know how to party. Their carnivals are possibly the best in the world for extravagant costumes and lively progressions. You can watch the genuine article or join your local carnival committee – both are fun things to do.

The samba reflects the lively nature of the Brazilian people, but you don't have to compete with them when you have your own little samba session – you have the freedom to dance how you feel.

When you need a break, make some cheese bread – it's delicious any time. And armchair caving can take you places you would never, ever explore yourself, but you can still enjoy the beauty of the underground world.

Carnival
Samba
Cheese bread making
Armchair caving

PORTUGAL

Do you know that half of the New World once belonged to Portugal? The Treaty of Tordesillas was signed in 1495. This divided the New World between

Spain and Portugal, Portugal having the eastern half. The treaty was in effect for 300 years, and Portuguese is still the national language of Brazil.

Portugal has a rich maritime history. Many famous explorers were Portuguese – sailors like Vasco da Gama (1460 - 1524) and Ferdinand Magellan (1480 - 1521), after whom the famous Magellan Straits around the southern tip of South America is named.

In many ways, Portugal is a relaxed country – the dances are less fierce than in neighboring Spain. Time-keeping can be elastic, and people tend to be tolerant and patient.

But their all-consuming passion, like in so many other countries, is football! Futebol, the beautiful game, has followers in every town, and perhaps the world's best player, Cristiano Ronaldo, is Portuguese. So it's not hard to start a conversation about football.

But crafts like embroidery and lace-making are popular, and so are water sports and their own traditional dancing.

FANDANGO AND FADO

Portuguese folk dancing illustrates courtship and marriage as well as local customs for each region. The dances are controlled and require practice and stamina to perform well. They are usually slower in pace than those of Spain. Famous dances include the fandango, chula, vira, and veranda.

Fado is the main music and song of Portugal. The tunes and lyrics are often sad and melancholy, but they do have an important traditional role. Fado is on UNESCO's "Representative List of the Intangible Cultural Heritage of Humanity." It is often played without dancing nowadays and offers a tiny peep at the past lives of poor and seafaring folk.

The pace of the dancing suits mature people and is a lovely way to spend an evening. Learning to fandango could be a relaxing, somewhat nostalgic hobby. You would need to find a group for the best experience, but there are online courses for you to pass a few hours in peace and tranquility in your own home.

There is a free online app called FandangoNOW that you can install onto your tablet or iOS. Why not try it and see?

BOBBIN LACE-MAKING

Portugal is renowned for its needlework crafts, embroidery, and lace-making. There are many craft fairs where you can examine and admire the gorgeous handiwork.

Lace-making has a history going back to at least 1616. It created a vital income for the area of Vila do Conde, but King João tried to ban lace from the ordinary people. The local lace makers were outraged and forced the king to withdraw his ban.

But the introduction of industrial lace-making in the 20th century forced a reduction in the home lace-making industry. As a result, the number of lace-makers declined from more than 500 to a mere 100 since the 1940s.

However, home lace-making was rescued by the introduction of annual fairs, handicraft centers, and contests. Lace-making it now alive and well in Portugal. There is even a statue of a bobbin lace maker in Vila de Conde, situated on the quay to commemorate those industrious ladies who made lace while their husbands were at sea. Yet another sculpture can be found in the fishing town Peniche, together with a museum dedicated to the craft of bobbin lace-making.

While lace-making is a skill, it can be learned, and lace-makers are often keen to share their knowledge. You may be lucky enough to find a group near you, which could be great for socializing as you craft a beautiful piece of lace. And lace is versatile and is not just for doilies, collars, and tableware; how about a lovely, lacy curtain to diffuse the sunlight? And, perhaps best of all, a lacy wedding dress?

How about starting your own lace-making group?

EMBROIDERY

Portuguese crafts are not confined to lace-making; their embroidery is also much sought after, and there are also expert knitters, crocheters, and rug makers.

Traditionally, their craftwork started in the nunneries and then as cottage industries to provide extra income for the fisher families and farmers. Each region has its own unique style.

Portuguese embroidery is rich in color and may involve a vast number of intricate stitches. White embroidery – using white thread on white cloth – is also popular now.

This hobby is another excellent opportunity for socializing. Still, it can just as equally be carried on at home, in the garden, or snug by the fireside on a cold winter's evening. And there are many books to give you ideas and instructions.

Embroidery can be a way to liven up an inexpensive blouse and make it something rather special. It can also be used to make jewelry, tableware, and gifts of all kinds.

CANOEING AND KAYAKING

With the coastline never far away, it's natural that windsurfing, kite surfing, and sailing are all popular. In fact, the largest wave ever surfed was recorded about 30 minutes north of Peniche.

But if you do not live near the coast, canoeing can be carried out on rivers as well as the sea. Canoeing is a popular sport both for the tourists and the locals in Portugal, and they have many top Olympians in canoeing and kayaking.

Less expensive than owning a boat, a canoe can be parked in the garage or hallway and brought out when you feel the need for some peace and quiet, a few moments of precious time for reflection, and even a workout – you might be surprised how much energy your legs burn; it's not just arm work.

Much of the kayaking in Portugal is done in two- or even three-seater kayak and is very safe. It is also a fantastic way to explore places that would otherwise be inaccessible.

It's a good idea to learn from an expert how to escape if your kayak turns over, which it will. The kayak roll is easy to master for a single-seater and could save you from a few very unpleasant moments.

PAINTBALL

Paintball is popular in Portugal. The country has several large paintball parks, and you probably have one near you as well, since this is a sport for all worldwide.

In Portugal, they have paintball parks in the open countryside, and the game is suitable for anyone over the age of ten and in reasonably good health. Very often, you play in teams.

Paintball uses guns that fire not bullets but balls of paint. This clearly shows where you have been hit. Cheating is not an option!

Strategy is all. Flanking maneuvers, duels, and retreats all play a part. The park will provide the equipment you need – markers, vests, color balls, as well as protective gear as required.

If the paintball park is good, there will be plenty of room for strategy; it's not just a game for the fastest and fittest. But this is something you can do with your grandchildren – they might have the energy, but you have the brains.

SUMMARY

The people of Portugal have a relaxed way of life, which is reflected in their traditional dances such as the fandango and their evocative music, the fado. The pace of the dances and music suit mature people who like to take their time and make the most of the pleasure.

But in active sports, the Portuguese excel in canoeing and kayaking, which is surprisingly energetic. It's a fine way to keep fit, and if there is a class near you, they will teach you how to get out of the upturned kayak with ease.

Another energetic activity for all ages (usually over the age of ten) is paintball; if you haven't tried it yet, that is a treat in store.

Portugal is famous for its beautiful lace and delicate embroidery. These crafts can be pursued at home alone and in friendly groups to catch up on all the local news.

Fandango and fado
Bobbin lace-making
Embroidery
Canoeing and Kayaking
Paintball

FIJI

Composed of over 300 islands in the South Pacific, Fiji enjoys a tropical climate and stunning scenery.

In the days of sailing ships, sailors tended to avoid Fiji, partly because of the treacherous waters but also because the inhabitants fiercely defended their territory. The men carved weapons, canoes, and knew how to use them.

But now, the tourist trade is the primary money earner, and many of the traditions continue to entice visitors. Grass skirts, war paint, and garlands of colorful flowers might greet the traveler. Even the treacherous waters are popular, some of the best waves for surfing are located near Fiji. The famous "Cloudbreaker" – an 18-foot wave, attracts surfers from afar.

Over the ground and under the sea, the scenery is spectacular. Many of the islands are tiny but packed with streams and waterfalls. The tropical jungle, the blue skies, and the coastal vistas make Fiji truly an enchanting place.

NATURE TRAILS AND GUIDED WALKS

The nature trails in Fiji are stunning. Fiji isn't just coral reefs and sandy beaches: there is a wealth of stunning scenery inland (although you are never far from the sea). Fiji's largest island, Viti Levu, has mountains, with Mount Tomanivi rising to 4,344 ft. Throughout the islands, there are nature trails to show off the very best areas and to allow you to meet the varied wildlife.

One example is the Lavena Coastal Walk. This three-hour hike takes in a coastline of black volcanic sandy beaches, rocky cliffs, waterfalls, and a village (where good manners mean you must wait to be invited in). The final waterfall can only be reached by swimming, so you might need a guide.

There are guided walks in most parts of the world, from ghost-spotting walks in London to a hike down the Parisian catacombs to "proper" nature trails. What is there on offer near you?

If you are like most of us, you may have traveled to far-off places to see their sights but may not have explored your local terrain. It might be worth seeing what is available closer to home.

You might even consider becoming a qualified guide to take others on a nature ramble or sightseeing around a historic building; volunteers are always needed. It is very satisfying to share your love and knowledge of places with other people.

LOVO – COOKING UNDERGROUND

An earth oven is one of the easiest and oldest methods of cooking. Little equipment is required, and if the power goes out, you can still produce a fabulous meal with just a fire to heat the stones and a hole in the ground.

Traditional cooking underground is huge in Fiji: families and restaurants all cook fish, chicken, and vegetables in improvised underground ovens. The result is succulent and delicious. Lovo is often the centerpiece of celebrations, weddings, and festivals. Fijians are experts in socializing, partying, and having a great time.

In Fiji, families will make a shallow hole in the ground and place heated stones at the base. Coconut husks are then used to line the oven. Palm leaves go on top of the hot stones, and this is followed by the vegetables, chicken, and breadfruit wrapped in more leaves and coconut fronds. This is covered with the soil and left to cook on its own for about an hour or maybe more. You can cook a huge amount of food at the same time with no risk of burning or overcooking. Just add sauces made from Polynesian fruit, chillis, and spices, and you can create your own Fijian feast.

Some of the restaurants use elaborate braiding of the banana leaves to enclose the food, and after being decorated with flowers, the results look and smell tantalizingly attractive.

Dessert can be cooked alongside the main course; for example, egg custard or vakalolo – which is coconut and cassava – steamed till soft and served with caramel sauce.

Just as in our more familiar barbecues, it's typically the men who prepare the lovo.

And there is no reason why you can't make your own lovo as long as you have access to a small piece of ground (and a shovel.)

Here's how to make your own earth oven:

Find a suitable place – one where there is no fire hazard.

1. Create a hole about two by three feet and a foot deep – keep the sides as vertical as possible.
2. Line the bottom and sides with flattish rocks. (If the stones are rounded, you may need a slightly bigger pit.)
3. Time to build a small fire to heat the rocks. Allow to burn for 45 minutes to an hour before it dies down.

Do not use wet or waterlogged stones, as the water trapped inside them might explode in the heat.

Your oven is prepared; now to put in the food, and if you do not have banana fronds and palm leaves, you can use tinfoil. Cover with the earth you have removed, and wait patiently or have a go at Fijian dancing to stimulate your appetite.

CRICKET

Cricket probably originated as a children's game in south-east England during the 13th century. They used a stone as a ball and a branch from the dense forest surrounding them at that time as the bat.

The game evolved: balls were no longer stone, and bats changed from a curved shape to a straight and wider one, often made from willow tree wood.

In the 19th century, English sailors carried their love of cricket to faraway places, including Fiji, where it is still a popular pastime today.

Fiji now has a men's team to play in the International Cricket Council (ICC) matches.

Although football is becoming increasingly popular, cricket still has a place in the hearts of many. Since it involves less physical contact than many other sports, it is suitable for all ages. But the masks and the hard balls and aggressive playing of some members can make this a risky game.

There is a saying, "It's just not cricket," which roughly means, "It's not fair," or "It's not the done thing."

You may prefer to play "French Cricket." This family game involves all members of the family playing at the same time, so there are no long periods of sitting out, waiting for your turn to bat.

SUMMARY

Fiji might not be very big, but the numerous islands possess incredible natural beauty, which, together with the generous and welcoming population, makes them an excellent tourist venue.

The activities in Fiji are as varied as the scenery, and many of them are great tourist attractions as well. Becoming a walking guide, lovo cooking underground, or taking up cricket are all hobbies you can pursue in your own country,

Nature trails and Guided Walks
Lovo underground cooking
Cricket

THE GAMBIA

The Republic of Gambia is the smallest country in Africa, but it is bursting with natural beauty, culture, and history.

A thin stretch of land only 30 miles wide, it borders the Gambia river, and is surrounded by the country of Senegal. One of the world's poorest countries, the Gambia used to be a center for the slave trade, and vestiges of that time still remain.

Today, the most significant industry is tourism. Gambians are proud of their country, and tourists will often end up with a young man to guide them to the markets and other places of interest. The markets are full of color, and sunhats, dresses, shirts, and wooden carvings of animals are all on display, plus so much more.

For the bird watcher, The Gambia is paradise. You can also visit a crocodile center and even stroke a croc if you are brave enough (they are well fed, so it is claimed they are not dangerous).

The 50 miles of scenic coastline allows one to relax in the sunshine, swim in warm waters, and generally chill out. So what hobbies do they have in The Gambia?

WOOD CARVING

Wood carving might be a hobby, but it is also a source of income. Every piece is unique – all hand-carved from local wood such as bombax, silk cotton, or mahogany.

Favorite items are local animals – antelope, crocodiles, giraffes, lions, elephants, monkeys, and turtles. But household objects such as bowls and dishes, musical instruments such as the balafon (a kind of wooden xylophone), and the local djembe drum are also commonly carved.

The method of carving has been handed down through the generations. First, a chunk of wood is chosen. Then the work starts using tools for deep cuts, with finer details added after the main shape has been created. Carving is never against the grain of the wood. Finally, the items are finished off with a coat of oil – linseed or walnut – to give a shiny, smooth finish that catches the light.

Wood carving is a hobby you could take up, although you are unlikely to reach the standard of these traditional Gambian carvings without a lot of practice. Choose a locally available softwood to start, attend a class, and be prepared for a steep learning curve.

But whittling away has always been something people loved to do while passing a few hours of time. You could improve on that and actually produce your own Gambian-style crocodile with a kink in its tail or a salad bowl that has a unique and endearing shape.

DRUMMING

In The Gambia, you can hear and see the djembe drums (pronounced "jem-bay") everywhere. They are an integral part of life, performing at weddings, births, and funerals, or just jamming on the beach for the delight of it.

The drums are constructed with great skill since the body is made from a single tree trunk, using those renowned Gambian carving skills, and the drum head is made from goatskin. The skin is made taut by tightening ropes around the body of the drum to tune it. Then, it is played with bare hands.

The djembe may have been in use as long ago as the 12th century. The name derives from words meaning "all gather together in peace," and this drum is not one used in war. With a little bit of practice, a djembe can produce many different sounds, and the player can tell an emotional story with this drum.

Djembes are not large drums – a medium-sized one might weigh about 20 lb – and by tradition, they are played by men. Women often play accompanying instruments, such as a kese kese, a kind of rattle.

The people of The Gambia grow up with the rhythm of the djembe, and when a group plays together, each may play their own individual tune, which interlocks to form a whole. At times, the melodies merge to form a united pattern and then diverge again to go their separate ways. It can be very complex and sometimes quite hard to follow for one unused to it.

Drumming makes a great hobby, especially if you are new to learning a musical instrument. It doesn't have to be complex, and it isn't hard to get an acceptable sound. You can play in a group or all on your own, but feeling the rhythm beating inside you as you drum can be intoxicating. Just remember that sound travels, and these drums were sometimes used to carry messages long distances.

SUMMARY

The Gambia is a small, poor country but is brimming with vitality. The carved animals are attractive and very collectible. It would be an interesting challenge for you to produce your own wood carving of an equal standard.

Gambians also make their own drums, and drumming is a marvelous way to let off steam. Their djembe drums can be found in many countries. Drumming is an easy way to enjoy performing regardless of your starting level of musical talent, using different types of drums for very different sounds.

Wood carving
Drumming

AUSTRALIA

Australia is BIG. It has both the vigor of new blood and some of the oldest traditions in the world.

This mix is recognized and celebrated, but conflicts between new arrivals and the Indigenous population have left their mark. The English penal colonies could be places of brutality, yet also gave opportunities to those able and lucky enough to benefit from them. We have wonderful artists, craftsmen, and great statesmen who emerged from those dark prisons.

The rugged landscape of vast, arid deserts has shaped many of the activities of the people who live there. There are also forests – now subject to fire as the climate heats up – impressive coral reefs, which are also in danger from warmer seas; the challenges are enormous. Still, the vitality of the people seems undaunted.

What follows is just a small selection of the hobbies Australians enjoy.

ROCK ART AND PEBBLE PAINTING

According to a book by Ian Wilson, "Lost World of the Kimberley," rock art in Australia may go back as far as 50,000 years. He describes Northwest Australia as a vast, arid, boulder-strewn place with hundreds of rock shelters, many with signs of paintings.

But the findings are confusing since the aboriginal people continue to paint the rocks, and they have a deeply religious significance. It isn't easy to be sure of how old the artwork is, even with technologies like carbon dating.

However a recent finding, a painting of a kangaroo, has been dated as 17,300 years old. The painting is 6'5" inches long and painted with red ochre on the roof of a rock shelter in Kimberley, in Western Australia.

But other findings suggest that rock art goes back further in Australia. In ancient times, travellers to Australia from Asia needed shorter sea trips than today, since the sea has risen, covering many of the smaller island stops in between.

The Kimberley kangaroo painting is remarkably similar to rock paintings in Southeast Asia, which have been dated to over 40,000 years old. So this does suggest a link. In Indonesia, the earliest animal painting we know of is a life-size depiction of a pig, which is 45,000 years old. But the oldest painting of all is a doodle in South Africa, dated 73,000 years ago.

In modern times, we have taken to painting pebbles and stones instead of caves. Rock or pebble painting needs nothing more than a decent rock, a lick of paint, and perhaps a coat of varnish to keep it looking nice. You may want to stick a piece of soft cloth underneath your finished pebble to protect any surface you put it on.

These painted pebbles make ingenious paperweights, or door stops, or just interesting ornaments. It's a hobby you can share with grandchildren – hunting for the right pebble is an integral part of the procedure, and kids are good at this.

You may wish to hide them in local parks, inviting people to photograph them and post them on social media. Recently, an artist painted pebbles depicting the Olympic winners.

Your own imagination is the only limit on how you create and use these modern rock paintings.

WATERCOLORS

Between 1804 and 1853, Britain transported roughly 76,000 convicts to Tasmania.

Some of these convicts were industrious; others were talented artists. Their works are not only beautiful to look at but are also of considerable historical interest. Photography was only beginning to be developed. These artists ranged from the habitually drunk but very talented, to the well-behaved model prisoner.

William Gould was very talented, when sober.

He was transported to Australia for stealing a coat, and during the voyage, he painted the officers' portraits. Once in Tasmania, he continued his way of petty crime, including the forgery of banknotes. He ended up working for a doctor/naturalist and painted fish, birds, and plants. Once freed, he continued to drink, and the high standard of his best work declined. But Gould's original Sketchbook of Fishes was of world significance, depicting some fish that are now extinct.

Then there was Thomas Bock, the "best portrait painter of them all." He was transported to Australia for giving his mistress drugs to induce an abortion. His job was preparing plates for banknotes! But his portraits, especially of young infants who had died, were sensitive and empathic.

Once free, he became interested in early photography and created beautiful portraits of the Indigenous people and the colonists – another valuable insight into the conditions of life among the early colonists and convicts.

Some of the convict paintings are a delight to gaze at, but they also offer a historical value. There were many more convict artists – but you don't need to be in prison to paint.

Watercolor painting is a beautiful way to pass your time and produce unique and lovely items to hang on your walls. You might also create cards to send to your friends or just enjoy the pleasure of painting.

Setting up your easel is the start of an adventure in vision. You see so much more when you are trying to put your interpretation down on canvas. There are many classes, internet study groups, and books to help you get started. You need a few tools and an old shirt to protect your clothes. There is no reason why you can't just start having a go yourself in the privacy of your home, but watercolor painting can also be a group activity.

Imagine meeting a few like-minded people, setting up your easels in a spot where the view is stunning, and having an experienced artist to help you create your own vision to take home with you.

CROQUET

Croquet originated in Ireland and was exported to England in 1852 under the name "crookey," which means a hooked stick. However, croquet arrived in Australia as early as 1881 and is now seen as an ideal game for men and women well into their 80s. Since the population of Australia is aging, the game is booming.

It's also a great family game, with youngsters joining in on equal terms. (It's also a great way to meet people of the opposite sex, according to Pippa Middleton.) The game is not particularly energetic or competitive, but it is full of strategy and tactics for serious players and requires considerable skill. It can be referred to as "chess on grass."

The game is played with a mallet to hit the balls through a series of hoops or "wickets." Nowadays, the balls are made not from wood but a composite plastic and the types of plastic used affect the durability, weight, and bounce of the balls. Games usually last about 30 minutes.

Croquet can be an excuse for a party. When Sean "Puffy" Combs was accepted onto the Hollywood Walk of Fame, he held a $2 million croquet party. People in Tasmania also played croquet at Christmas picnics, although tennis did oust the popularity of croquet for a while.

There are club-level games and international world championships. The UK, Australia, New Zealand, and the US compete for the MacRobertson Shield every four years.

All you need is a lawn, wickets, some balls, and mallets, plus a few people to play with, and you are set to go. Croquet is gentle exercise, a lot of fun, and an excellent hobby for all ages.

LOCAL HISTORY

Between 65,000 and 50,000 years ago, people journeyed to Australia from Southeast Asia to make it their home. They traveled as far as Tasmania; they penetrated the northern forests and even eked out a living in the arid central deserts. And they left their marks as described in the rock art of the shelters.

The traditions these early Australians established are among the oldest in the world. They have their music, their artistic remnants, and especially their spiritual heritage.

And then along came the Europeans.

First were the Dutch, then the famous James Cook from England, who charted the east coast. The first fleet of

British ships to arrive in Botany Bay came in 1788, and they started the first penal colony. More settlements were established, and Europeans penetrated far inland. The indigenous population was weakened by imported disease and by brutal conflicts with the settlers.

Gradually the prosperity of Australia increased, and modern Australia has welcomed over six million immigrants from every continent. As a result, trade is worldwide, and Australians have a wide range of museums and art galleries where people can begin to learn about their history and the history of this vast country.

The history of the Indigenous population is full of interest and a revival in the awareness of art, such as convict art and rock shelter paintings, which has stimulated both pride and belonging.

Local history can give you a feeling of belonging, too. Surprises may emerge from the local streets and villages, the local fields and woods, and the seas and rivers around you. There are often local history groups, meeting to explore your local places of interest. In addition, the internet and the local library often have a wealth of information just waiting for you to discover.

Local history might be allied to family history. The best is that you can do it even when it is pouring rain, and you don't want to venture outside.

SUMMARY

Australia is gigantic. The center of this enormous island is a hot desert, yet there are links to an ancient past. Rock art is deserving of respect, but you can make your own little link to the past by pebble painting. Another fascinating feature of Australia, especially Tasmania, is the lovely paintings that record the history of the early convict settlements; watercolor painting is one way to record your own history.

Indeed, local history can reveal some captivating and surprising facts about the place where you live. Local libraries often contain a wealth of information. And if, after all that "head work," you require a little gentle exercise with your friends or family, croquet is an ideal way to socialize without stress.

Australia has so much to offer, and I can only suggest a few ideas, but the links with the past, both ancient and more recent, make this a fascinating country. The chances are that you, too, live in an area where the past can speak to you.

Rock art and pebble painting
Watercolors
Croquet
Local history

LATVIA

The country of Latvia is a flattish plain filled with forests and the scent of pine trees. While there are some uplands to the east, grassy meadows and rolling hills make up most of the country. Yet, despite that plain description, Latvia has been voted the "most beautiful country in the world" several times.

Everywhere you go there are forests. They line the roads; they line the coast. There you find a rich harvest of lingonberries, bilberries, and mushrooms.

The Latvians do have a rather unusual sport – that of wife (or woman) carrying. These contests are thought to have originated in the 1800s when women were forcibly abducted. The Latvian style of carrying your wife is to have her hanging her head down your back with her legs over your shoulder, and you hang onto her lower legs and feet. They have special obstacle races, and the team with the fastest time wins.

But there are some more modern activities, so let's have a look at some of them.

MUSHROOM FORAGING

Latvians love mushrooms! Indeed, it is remarkable that there are any left in the forests after the autumn "shroomers" have been out foraging. But every year, many Latvians fill their fridges with the spoils from the woods – and it's free.

This hobby doesn't require a great deal of energy, so it is suitable for older people, who also bring their wisdom to the forest. It's healthy and takes you outside into the lovely countryside to fill the senses with pleasure and revitalize the brain cells.

Everywhere you look in the forests of Latvia, you can see people, heads down, straw hats on, carrying baskets filled with mushrooms. All you need is a knife and some knowledge of what you are collecting. Well, maybe more than a little...

The death cap, the deadliest of mushrooms, looks very similar to some edible mushrooms and is the most common source of mushroom poisoning. Death caps may have killed Emperor Claudius in 54 CE and Emperor Charles VI in 1740.

And even after the day exploring nature, there is the thrill of sorting your find, storing it, possibly even selling some of it, and the final triumph – mushrooms on toast for supper.

There are about 1,100 species of cap mushrooms, and you can eat three hundred of them, but most harvesters stick to the thirty or so types that they are familiar with. You may come across the golden-orange chanterelle, and you can be extra safe here since worms do not like them.

Then there are the boletus, which has no gills but instead has tubes for the spores beneath. They are excellent for drying and strong in taste. And there are so many more.

Here is a recipe for Latvian mushroom sauce:

Wild mushrooms, onion, ham (if you like ham), all chopped and fried together.

Then add sweet or sour cream with salt and pepper to taste. What could be simpler?

While mushrooming is a great hobby, it's best to start off in a group with someone who knows the types of mushrooms that are safe to eat. Many places have autumn mushroom foraging expeditions, and afterward, sorting your catch out in company is a great way to make friends. Of course, you also need a good reference book.

WEAVING

Archeology has unearthed some of the ancient crafts in Latvia, and weaving was of prime importance.

Around 2000 BCE, linen and wool were available in the early stone age, and different weaving techniques were developed, although we do not have traces of such early garments.

However, we do have bronze age fragments of clothing from the second to fourth century CE. Most of these are made from fleece, with traces of blue and red dyes still just discernible. These colors are often referred to in the Latvian folk songs or 'dainas.' You might also see yellow and dark brown. Because linen and hemp do not preserve well, they are most often found when combined with wool. And that meant some kind of weaving took place, with frames for the purpose, as long ago as Neolithic times.

Latvians also developed weaving that gave a tight and, therefore, warm fabric – needed in the cold dark winters. Latvian tribes were wearing plain fabrics of the "two-shaft" method by 100 CE, and by the 12th century, the "three-shaft" method, whereby diagonal lines were created, was also popular.

About this time, the horizontal weaving frame was introduced. Later on, weavers from Holland, France, and Germany introduced their techniques to the Latvians, who added them to their own traditional weaving techniques.

The Kurzeme cloths produced in the 16th and 17th centuries were highly regarded and a valuable export as well as a local commodity. Then, national costume and household textiles became increasingly crucial to Latvians, and their decorative weaving patterns are much admired.

Organized courses in weaving combine tradition and experience to enable others to produce fine artwork, and the State Museum preserves this Latvian heritage for us to enjoy.

Homemade textiles have value and uniqueness all of their own, and weaving as a hobby is entirely possible. The finished product makes lovely gifts, they can be sold, and most of all, they give you the pleasure of designing your own unique textiles.

You may be lucky enough to find local courses available, but in any case, there are many kits you can buy, videos you can watch and books you can read.

If you decide to try weaving, you will need some basic equipment:

1. A loom. This is the frame and comes in many sizes.
2. Shuttles.
3. A comb.
4. Tapestry needle.
5. Pair of scissors.
6. The thread.

To start off, you can use a piece of solid cardboard instead of buying a loom, but you will need a lot of yarn, so it is a great way to use up all those balls of wool you have never got around to knitting up.

Is weaving hard? It's as hard as you make it. The techniques are simple enough, but the patterns you make can be quite exciting and interesting.

DAINAS

These little four-liner folk songs allow us a glimpse into the past. There are over 1.2 million Dainas, and some were created over a thousand years ago. They recount daily life, celebrations, work, and reflections on people's lives.

Some Dainas celebrate Latvians' ancient pre-Christian gods and goddesses; others are about the mundane, everyday happenings, such as births where the mother figure appears to determine the child's fate. Like many religions, there is a sun goddess and a moon god.

Some Dainas mock; others are erotic. Some prepare a person for death, and of course, there are demons (who could be both good and bad) and an afterlife. In sum, they are a rich source of philosophy and beliefs.

Although the more usual heroic personages are absent, they allow us some insight into their legends and myths. Many Dainas have been translated into English.

I doubt that you can put so many rich thoughts into a four-liner, but it would be a unique way of keeping a diary and would undoubtedly make you think before you write. How could you put a day's experience into such a small poem, and does your Daina have a tune?

Writing your own Dainas could be a thought-provoking hobby and something to leave for posterity if you so wished.

POTTERY

We can date Latvian pottery to the Neolithic period; it is one of the country's most ancient forms of art.

Latvian pottery typically does not have patterns painted on but instead is a rich tapestry of solid colors and gradients. Traditionally, earth colors like brown and green were used, but modern artists have started inserting brighter colors onto their palettes. You can find mottled glazes and unusual shapes in the items produced nowadays.

Latgalian pottery

The region of Latgale is famous for its Latgalian pottery. Historically, Latgale produced pots for cooking, pots for storing sour cream, pots for fruit, and pots for honey, as well as pots for oil storage, pots for milk, and pots with handles for transporting – perhaps food for the workers in the fields?

Now the area produces modern ceramics, as well as some based on the ancient black ceramics from archeological discoveries, with little color.

Latgale pottery also includes figurines, candlesticks, decorative plates, and other contemporary items.

Pottery can be a fascinating hobby, but it does require some expenditure. The most expensive item is the kiln. Although there are ways of using your oven, especially if you are doing this with children, the results are often brittle and disappointing. But if you are prepared to invest in time for a course, and a little money for essential equipment, then you will be able to produce beautiful pots to adorn your home. Alternatively, you may be able to find a pottery studio that lets you take classes and use their kiln.

It's wise to learn from a professional potter before splashing out on your own. They can help you decide on the type of pottery you would like to make and guide you as to the equipment you will need, plus you might have a go at using the wheel!

SUMMARY

Latvia is a beautiful country of forests and more forests. No wonder foraging for mushrooms is so popular. This is an autumn activity you might enjoy – just be sure you know what you are collecting before eating it. Many places have mushroom foraging walks where you can discuss your findings with an expert.

Weaving is an ancient art, and if you want to try your hand, there are many kits available.

Pottery is another practical, ancient art. It makes a nice hobby but is best started by enrolling in a course and be guided by an experienced potter, as it is rather expensive to purchase your own materials and kiln. The feeling of the clay can be very therapeutic.

You might want to try your hand at writing a Daina. It could be another way to keep a journal.

Mushroom foraging
Weaving
Daina writing
Pottery

JAPAN

Are you interested in living a longer and healthier life? Why do you want to get up in the mornings? What pulls you out of bed each day?

What can we learn from Japan, home of the longest-living people, and where seniors enjoy an active, healthy life with purpose.

We will take our lessons from some key Japanese words: Ikigai, Hanami, Kintsugi, Kyudo, Origami, Haiku, and Onsen, which describe some very captivating hobbies.

IKIGAI

Ikigai is the reason why you get up in the morning. It's made of two words – "iki," meaning "life," and "gai," representing value. The word is not so much about the meaning of life as the joy in living. And since many of the oldest people in the world are Japanese, there must be some value in this concept.

Ikigai is different for different people. Work might be your ikigai (32% of Japanese consider this their ikigai), but it can equally well be related to family, to a love of travel, or to hobbies. Ikigai may appear to change as the person's life circumstances change, but when you look deeper, the change is superficial. The intrinsic values that drive the way a person experiences life remain the same: deep-seated and often unnoticed, they form the very core of a person's life.

So, let us look at some of the ways this attention to detail is a part of Japanese culture.

HANAMI

Hanami is the term used for the appreciation of cherry blossom trees. People take the time to sit and admire them and have parties to celebrate the brief span of time when the cherry blossom trees are in flower – between mid-March and early May.

Families and friends may gather to eat and drink under the blossom as the petals gently drift down upon them. Or someone may sit alone, lost in quiet contemplation.

Have you ever reached up to feel the super softness of the cherry blossom petals?

These cherry trees are known as Sakura, and they differ from ordinary cherry trees in that they are bountiful in pink and white blossom but do not produce fruit. Each tree is only in flower for a week or two, which reminds us of the transience of life and how precious every moment is.

This is an ancient tradition, going back hundreds of ears to the Naro period (710 – 794). Originally inspired by the Chinese, the "ume" plant was then admired, whose blooms lasted nearly two months. And then, the Japanese noticed the beauty of the Sakura, and this became their focus of appreciation. Poetry, literature, and philosophy have all been inspired by the blossom, both in Japan and China.

The bounty doesn't end in spring, for in autumn, people return to admire the turning of the leaves from green to red and gold. You might feel inspired by this to create a little space in a crowded life to imbibe the essence of nature. What beauty is around the corner in your neighborhood?

KINTSUGI

Kintsugi is a traditional Japanese craft where a broken vessel is repaired using a gold bonded resin. This fills the cracks and results in an even more beautiful item.

According to legend, this all started when a Japanese shogun sent a broken bowl to China to be repaired. The result was ugly – metal staples had been inserted to hold the pot together.

The local craftsmen thought they could make a better repair, and they experimented with new ways to mend the broken ceramic. Eventually, they discovered the gold bonded resin, and the process came to be known as kintsugi.

So impressed were the people with this new method of repair that they are said to have deliberately broken their pots to make them even more handsome when repaired with the gold-based resin.

If you look deeper into kintsugi, for the Japanese, it is a reminder that we are not perfect, to see beauty in that which is incomplete. In the process of healing ourselves, say after a break-up or a loss of some sort, we can learn to accept and celebrate our scars and imperfections and realize that we may have become even more unique and special with a newfound resilience. If you look closely at the art of kintsugi, the gold bond emphasizes the flaws within.

If you get the chance to visit Japan, be sure to search out this beautiful art form that may inspire you to start a creative project at home.

KYUDO

Japanese archery, or Kyudo, is a highly skilled sport, requiring dedication, practice, and more practice. Attention to detail and complete focus are needed to succeed, but all ages can participate.

The archers wear a specific costume: a kimono, very wide loose pants, and on their feet, tabo – socks with a thick sole and a separate part for the big toe.

The bows used are the longest in the world – up to 6 feet (2 meters) long – and they send arrows speeding out at 120 miles per hour (190 km per hour.)

Why are the bows so long? It's to stop them from breaking, as the longer the bow, the less force needed to draw it. But, given this length, the pull at the halfway mark of the bowstring is weak. So the archer does not pull at the halfway mark; they pull at a point one-third of the way up from the bottom. This is a sweet spot: the pull is strong, but the vibrations are weak, so a combination of greater power and accuracy can be achieved.

The accuracy can be astonishing. It's not just the physical power of the pull or the direction of the aim: it's a psychological preparation and mental state of mind that speeds the arrow to the target. The master Takeo Ishikawa demonstrated this spiritual training; he sent an arrow flying to the center of a distant target – in the dark!

The arrows preferred for use in competitions are the traditional bamboo arrows, made with great care. Carbon fiber arrows are often used in practice, but they are not as accurate as the traditional bamboo ones.

Every January, there is a long shot archery festival, and now Kyudo is practiced by thousands of people worldwide. A fascinating hobby, not for everyone but indeed a hobby to ponder.

ORIGAMI

Origami is a peaceful occupation possibly invented by the Japanese about 1000 years ago, but most likely had its roots in China. Now origami is a worldwide hobby, with special papers and many books of instructions. From paper airplanes sent by mischievous boys in the classroom to an activity for residents in a senior facility, origami can find a home anywhere.

Papermaking was invented in China around 105 CE and imported to Japan by Buddhist monks. By 610 CE, the Japanese were improving the quality of their paper, and it became suitable for origami, although it may not have been used as such back then. However, in 1680, a short poem by Ihara Saikaku mentions butterfly origami, revealing that the hobby of origami was well known. This is the short poem:

Rosei-ga yume-no cho-wa orisue.
(The butterfly in Rosie's dream would be origami.)

Originally, the art of folding probably applied to other materials – cloth, leather, even leaves. We still fold napkins in extravagant ways, and we may find our towels folded to resemble flowers or swans in upmarket hotels or onboard luxury liners, often just for the fun of it!

The value of origami also extends into teaching: it helps children to develop listening skills, take turns and cooperate, observe, follow directions, and to be patient.

Origami promotes confidence when the task is completed, helps to improve one's memory, and aids concentration. People with arthritis have found it helpful to release some of the tension from stiff fingers and strengthen the fine muscles in their hands.

Origami is calming and can be enjoyed alone or in groups, and is justifiably popular throughout the world. With a good book of instruction, Origami can be enjoyed in any part of the world. All you need is the required paper which you can always order online.

THE HAIKU

A haiku is a short, formal poem originating from Japan. It has a strict pattern and concentrates the mind wonderfully to ease out the essence of what you are trying to convey.

The traditional form has three phrases with a five-seven-five syllable pattern. The Japanese tend to write it on one line, whereas we use three lines in the West, as it's easier to read. The lines do not rhyme.

So the first line has five syllables, the second line seven, and the last line just five syllables again. Here is an example:

The Old Pond by Matsuo Basho
An old silent pond
A frog jumps into the pond—
Splash! Silence again.

And another haiku:

A World of Dew by Kobayashi Issa
A world of dew,
And within every dewdrop
A world of struggle.

How can one say so much with so few words? For all you word-lovers, writing a haiku could make an excellent hobby. I've started my collection of personally written haikus. But I'm not ready to share them with the world just yet.

ONSEN

You may be wondering how the Japanese relax. Japan is part of the Pacific Ring of Fire, where tectonic plates meet and volcanoes are born. So naturally, there are a great many hot springs. They are mentioned in Japan's oldest history book, written around 700 AD.

Many kinds of hot springs exist, from open-air examples to baths inside small hotels and hostels. The minerals in the water vary too, including calcium, sodium bicarbonate, sulfur, and iron. These minerals are absorbed through the skin while you lie back and relax, conferring many benefits to your health.

But entering Japan's hot baths is not the same as in most other countries. There is a strong and strict etiquette to be followed. This ensures your visit is pleasant and that every visitor can also have an enjoyable experience.

Originally men and women bathed naked together, but that is no longer always the case. Segregation of the sexes and swimming costumes or the special bathing "yakata" – a kind of kimono – is common, especially in tourist areas.

Cleanliness is still very much a part of the culture. You wash before entering the water. It is socially unacceptable to go in dirty or to drink alcohol there. But they make this easy by supplying well-stocked bathing stations where there is everything you need to get yourself spotless: soap, shampoo, taps, and buckets to ensure you wash off every trace of soap.

Then you can enjoy a relaxing hot soak in temperatures around 40°C. Even if the place is big, swimming is not encouraged.

Onsen has a dual purpose: cleanliness and relaxation.

You may not have an onsen close to you, but what other ways could you induce relaxation closer to home? I have seen beautiful spas in many places where one can go for a soak and relaxation. Many individuals have purchased a hot tub or infrared sauna to put in their homes for regular sessions to relax the body and mind. You may not consider this exactly a hobby, but one could participate in some form of relaxation on a regular basis.

SUMMARY

Japan melds the inner spirit and the outer life into a harmonious whole, and the life expectancy of the Japanese is longer than most.

Ikigai is a state of mind; it's your core value – why you get up in the morning. Finding yours can give you inner strength and serenity.

The Hanami, or cherry blossom, gives time for reflection in a natural setting to further this sense of calmness.

Kintsugi will restore your broken ceramics and make them even more beautiful.

Kyudo, Japanese archery, combines careful knowledge of the physical properties of the bow and the arrow –

another example of taking note of the detail. Archery is a fine hobby for some of us.

Origami is practiced worldwide – this can be a great teaching aid in patience and persistence as well as a nice little hobby for anyone.

Onsen is a calming way to relax using the hot springs, but you might have to make do with a warm bath, which is still relaxing. However, if there are hot springs near you, they are worth a visit.

When the evening comes, and you need a rest, why not try your hand at writing a haiku? It's not easy to put so few words together in a meaningful way. You might have to dig deep into your mind to construct a little masterpiece.

Ikigai – a state of mind
Hanami – appreciation
Kintsugi – beauty in imperfection
Kyudo – Japanese archery
Origami – paper folding
Haiku – short poems
Onsen – hot spring bathing

THE UNIVERSAL HOBBY

Our final hobby is to do nothing – nothing at all. But not in the passive, negative way our friend Harry (whom you met in the introduction) did nothing. There is a far better and different way to free your mind completely.

When you master this, you will find that your mind is more open to challenges, more confident in its ability to master them, and freer to engage in new activities.

It's like a painting. Generally speaking, one prefers to paint on a clean canvas, not cluttered with past efforts and mistakes. Your brain is the same. So, this is how you do it:

This is best done in a darkened room with you sitting comfortably and relaxed.

- Drop your shoulders to release tension and breath evenly and steadily.
- Now, light a candle. This should be unscented since you do not want to stimulate any of your senses.
- Gaze at the candle.
- Immerse your thoughts in the flame. Watch it as it flickers. Admire its many colors.
- Then – and this is the crux – if ANY thought comes into your mind, place it gently in a bubble and let it waft away. To start with, you may have to give it a gentle blow, but soon you will find you can just let the bubbles disappear on their own.

This can be incredibly hard to do.

At first, you might only be able to clear your mind for a moment, but with practice, you might extend the time to several seconds.

Some people practice candle gazing in many parts of the world. Some get so good at it that they can dispense with the candle and simply "candle gaze" without the candle. The brief moments of total control and a completely clear brain can reinvigorate them, resetting their inner self.

Why not try it and see how far you can get.

Candle gazing

FINAL THOUGHTS

You have traveled around the world, visiting new places and picking up new ideas along the way from people just like you.

While you might not be able to replicate all of these hobbies exactly, a few minor creative modifications are all it takes to turn even the most exotic activity into your new retirement pastime.

I hope that this book has been enlightening and given you ideas to follow and make your own. There is only this one life, and we all deserve to live it and enjoy it as much as we possibly can.

Don't be afraid to try something new. One of my favorite quotes is by Wayne W. Dyer and goes like this, "Go for it now. The future is promised to no one."

You might have ideas for some more unusual or interesting hobbies, and I would love to hear about them – and maybe include them in a future book. Please email me at: ravina@ravinachandra.com. I look forward to connecting with you.

People are inventive and exciting – I loved researching this book, and I hope you have enjoyed reading it.

INDEX

PSSSST, DON'T FORGET YOUR FREE GIFT!

In **'4 Simple Steps to Create Your Perfect Morning Routine,'** you will discover:

- What a **morning routine** is and why it is essential you have one
- Why having a morning routine will bring you **more focus, productivity, and purpose to your life**
- The secret of creating a morning routine using these **four components** that will **align with your core values**
- How a morning routine can elevate your life so that you may live **vibrantly**, whether you are seeking a companion, exploring new interests, or improving your health

Go to www.ravinachandra.com/books to get it NOW

REFERENCES

Australia

"Lost World of the Kimberley" by Ian Wilson

https://mail.google.com/mail/u/0/?pli=1#inbox/FMfcgzGkZkXNDrHppnwknFbDGnTQlgzm

https://learnantiques.com.au/historical-tasmanian-artists-part-2-four-australian-born-artists/

https://www.vanityfair.com/culture/2015/05/pippa-middleton-croquet-guide

Austria

https://blog.goodybeads.com/tutorial/diy-jewelry-with-swarovski-around-the-world-austria/

Belgium

https://archive.curbed.com/2014/1/2/10158982/frances-abandoned-chateau-miranda-is-a-ghost-hunters-paradise https://theculturetrip.com/europe/belgium/articles/belgiums-10-spookiest-spots/

Brazil

https://www.oliviascuisine.com/authentic-brazilian-cheese-bread/

China

https://fengshuinexus.com/feng-shui-rules/what-is-feng-shui/

https://luxurylaunches.com/travel/china-will-get-indoor-waterfall-almost-high-niagara-falls.php

https://www.familysearch.org/blog/en/chinese-family-tree-jiapu/

https://www.calligraphy-skills.com/italic-lettering.html

Denmark

https://www.legoland.dk/en/

https://www.lego.com/en-us/aboutus/news/2019/october/lego-campus-grand-opening/

Fiji

https://www.motherearthnews.com/real-food/how-to-build-your-own-earth-oven-zmaz78jazbur

France

https://www.chartreuse.fr/en/visites/chartreuse-cellars-in-voiron-special-english-guided-tour/

https://www.vinotrip.com/en/images lavender fields

Germany

https://www.geocaching.com/blog/2013/02/celebrating-two-million-geocaches-list-by-country/

https://www.postcrossing.com/blog/2014/05/15/toyvoyagers

Greece

https://learn.oliveoilschool.org/

https://www.mysteriousgreece.com/mood/activities/

https://www.ornithologiki.gr/en/

Italy

https://www.gonomad.com/1766-italian-hand-gestures-in-conversation

Latvia

https://en.wikipedia.org/wiki/Daina_(Latvia)

New Zealand

https://www.aucklandforkids.co.nz/toys-games/best-family-board-games/

https://www.rnz.co.nz/concert/programmes/musicalive/audio/2018713707/the-big-sing-2019-gala-concert-first-half

Portugal

http://EzineArticles.com/8965247

Singapore

https://www.capitalsenior.com/virtual-reality-allows-seniors-to-experience-a-whole-new-world-right-at-their-fingertips/

https://www.barfboutique.com/lasticos

https://mapletreemedia.com/famous-blog-in-singapore/

Thailand

https://mymodernmet.com/soap-carving-narong-thai/

https://www.wikihow.com/Make-a-Soap-Carving

http://woodcarvingillustrated.com/blog/2018/04/05/carving-a-soap-flower/

The Netherlands

https://cheesemaking.com/products/edam-cheese-making-recipe

https://www.kaasworkshops.nl/en/make-cheese-or-butter/

The UK

https://www.nationaltrust.org.uk/

https://www.english-heritage.org.uk/

https://www.heritagetrustnetwork.org.uk/about-us/areas/northern-ireland/

https://www.historicenvironment.scot/

https://cadw.gov.wales/

FROM THE AUTHOR

Thank you so much for reading *101 Ways to Enjoy Retirement*. Please don't forget to write a brief review at Amazon or wherever you purchased this book. I am grateful for all feedback and your review will help other readers decide whether to read this book too.

Interested in staying in touch to hear about any of my future books or projects? Would you like the opportunity to work with me directly in a personalized 90-day coaching program?

Contact me at ravina@ravinachandra.com

or visit www.ravinachandra.com

IMAGE CREDITS

Introduction

Active Senior photo courtesy of mgfoto, Pixabay.com, Pixabay License

Australia

1399 (Kangaroo) photo courtesy of Andrew Bertuleit, Pixabay.com, Pixabay License

Watercolor Map of Australia. Watercolour Illustration photo courtesy of undrey's images, Pixabay.com, Pixabay License

Austria

Accordion photo courtesy of tellmemore000, Pixabay.-com, Pixabay License

Salzburg, Austria photo courtesy of sorincolac, Pixabay.-com, Pixabay License

Volkstheater in Vienna Austria at Night photo courtesy of and.one, Pixabay.com, Pixabay License

Belgium

Hot Air Balloons courtesy of JMartinPhotography, Pixabay.com, Pixabay License

Patchwork photo courtesy of philipimage, Pixabay.com, Pixabay License

Brazil

Cave, Ubajara National Park, Brazil photo courtesy of tunart, Pixabay.com, Pixabay License

Favela houses in Brazil photo courtesy of Aliaksei Skreidzeleu, Pixabay.com, Pixabay License

Pao de Queijo photo courtesy of AndreaGoldschmidt, Pixabay.com, Pixabay License

Canada

Curling Woman photo courtesy of nojustice, Pixabay.com, Pixabay License

Free outdoor library photo courtesy of ImageGolf, Pixabay.com, Pixabay License

Park RV in Camp Site photo courtesy of anonymous, Pixabay.com, Pixabay License

China

Caligraphy practice photo courtesy of BVBeckman, Pixabay.com, Pixabay License

Chinese Calligraphy photo courtesy of SteveAllenPhoto, Pixabay.com, Pixabay License

Feng Shui balance photo courtesy of zeleno, Pixabay.com, Pixabay License

Rain vortex at Jewel Changi Airport, Changi, Singapore photo courtesy of William Chng, Pixabay.com, Pixabay License

Denmark

Nyhavn photo courtesy of SuppalakKlabdee, Pixabay.com, Pixabay License

Runic Stone photo courtesy of Plougmann, Pixabay.com, Pixabay License

Untitled lego photo courtesy of Efraimstochter, Pixabay.-com, Pixabay License

Fiji

Fijian Food Lovo in Fiji Islands photo courtesy of chameleonseye, Pixabay.com, Pixabay License

Tropical beach photo courtesy of Nurture, Pixabay.com, Pixabay License

France

champagne photo courtesy of lea dubois, Pixabay.com, Pixabay License

vineyard and medieval church in Alsace, France photo courtesy of Milena Pigdanowicz-Fidera, Pixabay.com,

Pixabay License

Woman riding on an adult tricycle photo courtesy of Creatas, Pixabay.com, Pixabay License

Gambia

Djembe players photo courtesy of peeterv, Pixabay.com, Pixabay License

Flag of Gambia photo courtesy of enigma_images, Pixabay.com, Pixabay License

Germany

BERLIN, GERMANY photo courtesy of Aliaksei Skreidzeleu, Pixabay.com, Pixabay License

Dramatic sunset over river photo courtesy of Britus, Pixabay.com, Pixabay License

Garden Gnome photo courtesy of anela, Pixabay.com, Pixabay License

Greece

Greece photo courtesy of oversnap, Pixabay.com, Pixabay License

Olive Grove Tree Greece photo courtesy of Kloeg008, Pixabay.com, Pixabay License

Italy

Cinque Terre, Italy photo courtesy of Walkerssk, Pixabay.-com, Pixabay License

Hand gestures photo courtesy of mycan, Pixabay.com, Pixabay License

Mosaics in Ravenna, Italy photo courtesy of Flavio Valenari, Pixabay.com, Pixabay License

Japan

Kintsugi Japanese antique ceramic bowl photo courtesy of Marco Montalti, Pixabay.com, Pixabay License

Origami photo courtesy of paolaroid, Pixabay.com, Pixabay License

Young woman looking at cherry blossoms at hanami party photo courtesy of Santosh-k, Pixabay.com, Pixabay License

Latvia

Colorful pottery photo courtesy of inguuna, Pixabay.com, Pixabay License

Exotic mushrooms photo courtesy of Langan, Pixabay.com, Pixabay License

Famous square in old Riga city, Latvia photo courtesy of gorsch13, Pixabay.com, Pixabay License

New Zealand

Beekeeper Controlling Beeyard photo courtesy of Kzenon, Pixabay.com, Pixabay License

Crochet baby booties photo courtesy of gojak, Pixabay.com, Pixabay License

Portugal

Beautiful fado singer performing with handsome Portuguese guitarist, Portugal photo courtesy of Jacek_-Sopotnicki, Pixabay.com, Pixabay License

Bobbin lace manufacturing courtesy of Mercedes Rancano Otero, Pixabay.com, Pixabay License.

Traditional historic facade in Porto decorated with blue tiles, Portugal photo courtesy of Mirifada, Pixabay.com, Pixabay License

Singapore

Colorful knitting from recycle plastic bag photo courtesy of prapassong, Pixabay.com, Pixabay License

Panorama of marina bay sand, garden by the bay and Singapore flyer photo courtesy of Pasu Lo-utai, Pixabay.-com, Pixabay License

Thailand

Antique Thai Buddha amulets in an amulet market, Thailand photo courtesy of enviromantic, Pixabay.com, Pixabay License

Soap Carving Flower photo courtesy of Praiwun, Pixabay.-com, Pixabay License

The Netherlands

traditional cheesemaking photo courtesy of nullplus, Pixabay.com, Pixabay License

Traditional dutch windmills and houses photo courtesy of Olena_Z, Pixabay.com, Pixabay License

United Kingdom

British Tea photo courtesy of Upyanose, Pixabay.com, Pixabay License

Untitled (Castle) photo courtesy of Graham_H, Pixabay.-com, Pixabay Licensething

Universal Hobby

Candle Lit in Black Background photo courtesy of Jordi C, Pixabay.com, Pixabay License

Printed in Great Britain
by Amazon

d49a19cc-da74-4fff-8c26-f1bf5dd41049R01